"Josh and Gary have identified and solved for a real gap in the space of negotiation theory and training. By taking a team and systems approach to enhancing the skill set for the organization, not just the individual, they tap into all of the alignment and reinforcing mechanisms necessary to drive meaningful and sustainable behavior change and organizational impact."

Stephen Frenkel, *Voyager Executive Consulting, LLC,*
Senior Director of Organizational Development at Cigna

"A fresh look at the elements of successful, repeatable negotiation competence for organizations. By focusing on the organization and not just individual negotiator's skills, this book is a real contribution to the field. Graphics, summaries, and real-world examples give added value."

James E McGuire, *JAMS, Mediator and Arbitrator*

"Most view negotiation as occurring between two disputing parties. Sometimes, in online dispute resolution, technology serves as a kind of 'Fourth Party,' assisting in some way to manage communication. *Strategic Negotiation: Building Organizational Excellence* expertly points us in a new and valuable direction by alerting us to the powerful influence of the organization on the participants."

Ethan Katsh, *Director at National Center for Technology and Dispute Resolution at the University of Massachusetts, Amherst*

"Joshua and Gary have developed a holistic and systemic negotiation approach that aims to connect individual training with organisational and institutional needs. Their Negotiation Capability Model is a useful tool to broaden the field of negotiation to help us focus on the connections between individual skills and abilities through alignment with strong organisational frameworks."

Enda Young, *Founder of the Negotiation and Influencing Programme at Queen's University Belfast and Managing Director of Mediation, Northern Ireland*

"Negotiation doesn't happen in a vacuum. Furlong and Gordon recognize this and show the reader how organizations can set the stage for negotiation success by taking a holistic approach to the practice. This book is a valuable addition to the bookshelves of negotiators and organizational leaders alike."

David Wagner, *University of Oregon Professor of Management*

"This book changed my perspective on how to train negotiators. Rather than focusing on building the skills of an individual, I learned how important the context of the organization is to set them up for success. The Negotiation Capability Model brings a clear, specific, and actionable framework to create the right environment for negotiators to truly succeed."

Mary Miksch, *Director of Organizational Development and Training at Neil Kelly Company*

"If any organisation wants to turbo-charge their negotiations then this book provides the insight. This book allows any organisation to self-assess its own maturity to develop a unique roadmap for evolving both firm and individuals over time - a must-read for individual professionals and business leaders alike!"

Cosette M. Reczek, *Founder, Permuto Consulting*

"This book offers a strong argument and path for improving your organization's efficacy, and bottom line, by improving foundational negotiation capabilities. As an engineer, the structure and applicable model resonated loudly for the organizations I work with!"

Peter Cheimets, *Lead Business Developer at the Smithsonian Astrophysical Observatory*

Strategic Negotiation: Building Organizational Excellence

Empowering organizations to thrive, this book provides a clear diagnostic framework with specific approaches and processes that leaders can use to build a negotiation function that will succeed each and every time.

Negotiation is a required skill and a core competency, but most organizations focus exclusively on individual negotiation skills and abilities and pay little attention to the internal culture and environment that shapes and guides these individuals. This book takes a dramatically different approach to building success in each and every negotiation, producing results that align with organizational strategy at all levels.

Professionals in sales, procurement and supply chain, human resources, change management, mergers and acquisitions, contracts, start-ups, construction partnering, and training consultants and students of business and law will value a text that understands how to build negotiation skills and capability across the organization by aligning individual skills with an evidence-based approach that actually works.

Joshua A. Gordon, JD, MA, is an experienced educator, arbitrator, negotiator, facilitator, consultant, and organization capability builder. Joshua is Faculty at the University of Oregon Lundquist College of Business where he teaches courses on negotiation, conflict management, law, and sports business. He has helped build organizational negotiation capability and served as a strategic negotiation advisor across just about every industry and sector. He is the co-author of *The Sports Playbook: Building Teams That Outperform Year After Year*, Routledge, 2018.

Gary T. Furlong, LL.M BA, is Chartered Mediator (CMed) and holds his Master of Laws (ADR) from Osgoode Hall Law School. He is the author of *The Conflict Resolution Toolbox*, Second Edition, John Wiley and Sons, 2020; the co-author of *BrainFishing: A Practice Guide to Questioning Skills*, FriesenPress, 2018; and the co-author of *The Sports Playbook: Building Teams That Outperform Year After Year*, Routledge, 2018.

Strategic Negotiation: Building Organizational Excellence

A Roadmap to Harnessing the Power of Alignment

Joshua A. Gordon
Gary T. Furlong

Routledge
Taylor & Francis Group

NEW YORK AND LONDON

Designed cover image: Getty//Digital Storm

First published 2023
by Routledge
605 Third Avenue, New York, NY 10158

and by Routledge
4 Park Square, Milton Park, Abingdon, Oxon, OX14 4RN

Routledge is an imprint of the Taylor & Francis Group, an informa business

© 2023 Joshua A. Gordon and Gary T. Furlong

Library of Congress Cataloging-in-Publication Data
A catalog record for this title has been requested

ISBN: 978-1-032-15378-0 (hbk)
ISBN: 978-1-032-15377-3 (pbk)
ISBN: 978-1-003-24385-4 (ebk)

DOI: 10.4324/9781003243854

Typeset in Bembo
by Apex CoVantage, LLC

Contents

Foreword

Leave it to Joshua A. Gordon and Gary T. Furlong to introduce us to negotiation as a team sport. Buckle your seat belts and get ready for an innovative, problem-solving approach to win–win.

These two authors have written a valuable book everyone needs to own. Joshua A. Gordon is a former athlete and industry and academic leader in the intersection of sport and conflict resolution alongside his innovator status in all things negotiation. Gary T. Furlong is a leader in mediation and researches the relationship between team performance and dispute resolution processes. In their previous publication, *The Sports Playbook*, they focused on building successful sports teams. In this book, they pivot using their expertise in sports and business to innovate the field of negotiation.

Traditionally, the art of negotiation was considered a skill-based competency with books and courses used to train individuals. As athletes quickly learn, training alone does not lead to excellent performances. It requires clearly outlining the desired outcomes and building sustainable relationships with coaches, teammates, trainers, sponsors, events, and competitors. The same is true for companies and organizations who want to succeed in the rapidly changing world. Josh and Gary offer a modern approach with an organizational perspective to building negotiation competencies. I was particularly impressed with the introduction of the Negotiation Capability Model (NCM) and the Negotiation Assessment Tool (NAT). The NCM serves as a guide by making access to the information provided in the book easy to reference for future use in your business or organization.

Having spent three decades at Nike, and my last decade at the University of Oregon, I witnessed countless opportunities to utilize a new approach to traditional negotiation techniques. As a former Nike executive with assignments in Hong Kong, Japan, Thailand, and Korea, my days were full of complex negotiations on projects and products with internal teams and external partners. In 2002, as the general manager of Nike's Liaison office in Bangkok, Thailand, it was reported to us that hundreds of workers from the far north of Thailand were unhappy with a factory closure and they had traveled to Bangkok to demonstrate in front of the government buildings and Nike's office. Although the factory had not manufactured any Nike products for two years, the workers knew and trusted the Nike brand to find a resolution. And Nike helped in the government negotiations, which ended with a positive outcome of jobs for the workers in another location, as well as providing transportation for the workers to return to their homes.

I could have used Josh and Gary's tested negotiation roadmap. If this book would have been available 20 years ago, it would have served as a practical reference guide and likely gotten us to the resolution faster. With its design-thinking approach, this book provides negotiators with the ability to maximize each step in the process to guide teams toward win-win solutions. From the boardroom to the classroom, leaders will find value in this new team approach to negotiation.

Thank you, Josh and Gary, for introducing us to the team sport of negotiation with skills that everyone can learn and that provide benefits to every organization that implements them.

Ellen Schmidt-Devlin
Executive Director of Lundquist College of Business Portland Programs at the University of Oregon and former Nike, Inc. senior executive

Acknowledgments

Josh: I wish to thank the many mentors I have had since my immersion in ADR and negotiation in the early 1990s, including Janet Rifkin, Leah Wing, Ethan Katsh, Albie Davis, James McGuire, Eben Weitzman, Susan Opotow, Larry Susskind, Dwight Golann, Marc Greenbaum, David Matz, Bradley Gordon, and Gail Packer; my co-author, Gary T. Furlong, for being a tremendous collaborator, partner, and friend over the past decade since I first sent you a random email about some of the creative uses I had found for one of your previous texts; my colleagues at the University of Oregon, for continuing to provide an enriching home base to keep me challenged and forever in learning mode; and finally, my wife, Renee Gordon, and our daughter, Joelie Gordon, for not calling me crazy too many times for taking on such an endeavor amid a global pandemic.

Gary: I would like to thank my friend Jim Harrison, Rick Russell and the team at Agree Inc., and my co-author Joshua A. Gordon, who has been nothing short of fantastic to work with and spend time with. The deepest thank you to my family—Callan, Tess, and my partner in everything, Ronalda Jones.

About the Authors

Joshua A. Gordon, JD, MA, is an experienced educator, arbitrator, negotiator, facilitator, consultant, and organization capability builder. He is faculty at the University of Oregon Lundquist College of Business where he teaches courses on negotiation, conflict management, law, and sports business. He serves as the Faculty Athletics Representative (FAR/"Dean of Athletics") helping negotiate complex issues related to intercollegiate athletics. He earned his bachelor's degree in psychology and sociology from the University of Massachusetts at Amherst, a master's and a graduate certificate in dispute resolution from the University of Massachusetts Boston, and his juris doctorate from Suffolk University Law School. He is an arbitrator for the Court of Arbitration for Sport (CAS), a mediator for the Federation Internationale de Football (FIFA), is on the editorial board for LawInSport, and the founding practitioner of the Sports Conflict Institute.

Joshua has helped build organizational negotiation capability and served as a strategic negotiation advisor across just about every industry and sector. He is the co-author of *The Sports Playbook: Building Teams That Outperform Year After Year*, Routledge, 2018.

Gary T. Furlong, BA, LLM (ADR), C.Med, has extensive experience in negotiation, mediation, alternative dispute resolution, and conflict resolution. Gary is a Chartered Mediator (C.Med) and holds his Master of Laws (ADR) from Osgoode Hall Law School. He is the author of *The Conflict Resolution Toolbox*, Second Edition, John Wiley and Sons, 2020; he is the co-author of *BrainFishing: A Practice Guide to Questioning Skills*, FriesenPress, 2018; and the co-author of *The Sports Playbook: Building Teams That Outperform Year After Year*, Routledge, 2018. He was awarded the McGowan Award of Excellence by the ADR Institute of Canada.

Gary has coached, facilitated, and supported negotiators in a wide range of industries including construction, contract management, dispute resolution, and labor relations. He frequently consults with organizations on ways to improve their outcomes through the negotiation process. He has taught negotiation skills for over 30 years.

Gary is a past president of the ADR Institute of Ontario, and is currently a distinguished fellow of the International Academy of Mediators (IAM), a fellow of the Canadian Academy of Distinguished Neutrals (CADN), and an advisory board member of The Sports Conflict Institute.

Introduction—The Power of Alignment

There have been over a thousand negotiation books published in the last 50 years alone. Why would we even consider adding another negotiation book to that total?

The reason is simple. Virtually every negotiation book published, every negotiation training course offered, and every organization that relies on skilled negotiators treats negotiation as an individual skill set. Negotiation is predominantly seen as an innate ability some people have and some people don't. Or it is seen as a learnable skill set that anyone, with extensive training, can improve—if only we have the right individuals. And once we have the right individuals—gifted or well-trained—we will have effective and successful outcomes to our negotiations. Problem solved.

Figure i.1 Individual Skills

Individuals with strong negotiation skills and abilities are indeed important. Skill and ability are the price of admission. But having the right skills is only one piece of the puzzle, and it's not even the largest piece. We have to have all pieces of the puzzle in place if we're to complete the picture, if we are to have strong and sustained success in the negotiation process.

While the focus on individual skills and abilities is important, overfocusing on the individual has obscured the other side of the coin—the organizational competencies and structures that need to be in place and aligned to ensure repeatable success at the bargaining table.

DOI:10.4324/9781003243854-1

Figure i.2 Individual and Organizational Skills

This book delivers this missing link by identifying the organizational capabilities that are needed to create repeatable and reliable success in every negotiation. We show how negotiation is actually a team activity, a set of critical organizational competencies that form a foundation and framework that enable individuals to succeed at the table. Over and over. This book will help create alignment between an organization's strategy and resources and the application of each individual's skills and abilities.

This alignment is what brings strength, resilience, and repeatable, adaptable negotiation success, over and over. This alignment is the true form of negotiation power at the table.

Negotiation Myths We All Know and Love

The field of negotiation is a wonderful place, full of magical beliefs and wishful thinking. Myths abound in the field, unencumbered by reality, and most serve to limit success for organizations and individuals alike. Some of the most powerful myths include the following:

- Negotiation is about the negotiator themselves, and successful negotiators are people who have a unique ability, a talent, a charisma, something almost magical about them. Or,
- Negotiation is a contest, a battle of wits, a winner/loser game like Texas hold 'em poker or most sporting events. Or worse, it is seen as war, a form of combat, led by a heroic action figure imposing their will on others at the bargaining table. Or,
- Regardless of everything else, negotiation in the end is about power, about winning, or at the very least getting more than the other party gets at the table. It's about gaining and exercising power above all else,

These myths are reflected in the many negotiation book titles that have sold millions of copies, including:

- *48 Laws of Power*—amoral, ruthless, cunning approaches[1]
- *Bargaining for Advantage*[2]

- *Secrets of Power Salary Negotiating*[3]
- *99 Negotiating Strategies: Tips, Tactics and Techniques*[4]
- *Never Split the Difference*—a former FBI Negotiator's book[5]
- *You Can Negotiate Anything!*—from the "World's Best Negotiator"[6]
- *Good For You, Great For Me*[7]

Power, cunning, advantage, tips, tricks and tactics, winning—virtually every book reinforces the idea that negotiation is all about learning the skills to out-negotiate the other party. Even books that promote a collaborative approach to negotiation also promote a very individual-centric approach to the negotiation process.

These books might as well be given titles that honestly reflect the myths they perpetuate, such as:

- Harry Potter's Negotiation Spell Book—Lucky Charms for Winning!
- The Terminator—Intimidate Your Way to Success
- Winning Negotiations and Influencing People—Charisma Gets Deals
- Live by These Clever Tricks, Die by Other Clever Tricks
- The Art of the Deal

Why Do These Myths Persist?

There are a number of reasons why these myths persist.

First, in any complex activity, we like to identify an individual with the outcome—and we like to either celebrate or shoot (as the case may be!) the messenger. In team activities, for example, we tend to find a single person to either give credit or blame. The CEO appears to make every decision, regardless of how large the organization is. The quarterback or the coach is the only reason the team wins or loses.

Or worse, we identify specific actions or behaviors and link these with success, turning them into something bordering on superstition. Athletes, for example, are famous for idiosyncratic routines they perform before every match or race as necessary to winning.

Second, popular culture has reinforced this belief, often portraying strong, rugged, clever people out-negotiating their opponents using sheer will, force, cleverness, or intimidation to get what they want (movies like *The Negotiator, The Wolf of Wall Street, Lincoln, The Devil's Advocate* all portray these beliefs). It's great theater but wildly misleading.

Third, organizations have accidentally supported these myths. Often looking for short-term solutions, companies bring in individuals with proven success as negotiators and then give them free reign—provided they deliver the goods. Whether they succeed or not, the underlying approach is focused on finding individuals who can "get the job done." Organizations also support this myth by thinking that extensive negotiation skills training is all that's needed. While certainly not a bad thing, negotiation training alone will rarely result in ongoing success at the table.

The results of operating based on these myths are seen in many ways. The most common are the following:

- Individuals are left to their own devices, often without the needed support, to sink or swim. If negotiations fail, send them on more training. If they fail more than once, change the negotiator.
- When hiring, hire "tough" negotiators to heroically defend the interests of the organization at any cost. This approach often ends up with the negotiator seeming to win the battle but often losing the war—and, eventually, the client. With this approach, unintended consequences for the organization abound.
- Even when deals are made, the negotiated outcomes often fail to support the overall organizational strategy. When individual negotiators pursue the short-term goal of the "best deal" today, the "deal" tail may end up wagging the "strategic" dog.
- In almost all cases, organizations fail to measure success at the bargaining table, and with little data to assess the outcomes of their negotiations, it becomes easy to continue relying on and living by these myths.

The Fallacy of Training

Let's start with the value of individual negotiation skills and where they fit. Individual skills, long the paradigm and focus for negotiation success, remain a necessary part of the foundation for effective negotiation capabilities. Individual skill, however, is far from sufficient for achieving consistent success at the table.

Over the years, a familiar inquiry has come our way. An organization reaches out and wants us to deliver a one-day or multi-day negotiation training course for their employees. They believe that giving their staff some basic knowledge and skills will quickly change the outcome of their organization's negotiations. These requests vary in size, scope, and context, but the request and their beliefs are clear—train our individuals, give them good negotiation skills, and suddenly all will be good. In reality, success often requires a deeper exploration of the goals of the organization and the objectives that the negotiation process is aiming to achieve.

For example, a custom home builder reached out to an expert negotiation trainer seeking to schedule training for their sales team. Sales numbers were lagging, as were overall customer satisfaction numbers, and they wanted to improve the individual negotiation skill set of their sales team with the idea that improving these skills would drive sales. It was a logical (and well-intended) request and intuitively it seemed like a good idea. However, they had been down this road before, had conducted training before, and saw little impact on their results after the training. Their conclusion, quite simply, was that they needed better training. Possible, but not likely. Instead, they agreed to look at their current organizational processes and tools and how they were currently guiding and supporting the sales and negotiation function. First, they learned that from the very start of the sales process they were failing to identify the important interests of their customers, customers who were purchasing high-end custom homes. Instead of training as a first step, they developed a specific set of goals and objectives that salespeople needed to achieve with each customer, starting with identifying their unique needs and interests. Almost immediately, they were able to capture key information about their potential customers, allowing them to tailor options and solutions to meet those needs. Every salesperson was held accountable by the organization for implementing this new focus and approach. Not only did their sales numbers skyrocket, they also went on to win customer satisfaction awards, year after year. With the changes they made at the organizational level, and without additional training, individual salespeople could focus their skills more effectively and deliver the desired results.

While we regularly deliver training that gives people leading-edge knowledge and important skills for negotiation, the belief that simply offering training will solve the problem is rarely borne out. In other words, training by itself is rarely the solution. Organizations want to be good at negotiating—in fact, they need to be. So, why isn't training the answer?

There likely is no single answer as to why training rarely improves outcomes, but there are some identifiable themes. The reasons can be categorized broadly as either tactical failures or strategic failures. Tactical failures include "poor quality training, lack of follow-through after the training, and lack of clear and appropriate training objectives to provide direction and focus."[8] Strategic failures are different and include things like

> lack of alignment with business strategy and needs, failure to recognize non-training solutions, regarding training as an event, participants not held accountable for results, failure to prepare the job environment for knowledge transfer, lack of management reinforcement and support, lack of commitment and involvement from executives, and other organizational barriers to success.[9]

Some of these training-related barriers are relatively easy to resolve. Yet if training isn't the whole problem, then it surely can't be the whole answer. Unfortunately, even if training is excellent and avoids the tactical failures, the outcomes around negotiation that organizations are seeking won't happen, simply because of the strategic failures. In other words, there are core organizational capabilities that must be put in place to support the newly trained individuals. The organization must be fully aligned and tangibly supporting the negotiation knowledge and skills learned in the training. Without this alignment, the knowledge and skills simply won't transfer.

Hopefully, this point is crystal clear—individual skill and effort alone will not transform the organization; training by itself will change very little. This is true even of the most dynamic, evidence-based training programs. Training must be done in the context of each specific organization, its unique values, goals and direction, and anything less will likely lead to the participants saying, "Great training! Too bad it won't work *here*." Many participants have told us, "Thanks for the great information, but nothing is going to change when I return to work on Monday."

While training isn't the only solution, it is still certainly one piece of the puzzle, however large or small. For an organization to be truly successful at the bargaining table, we will need to see the full picture.

The Power of Alignment

This book is about finishing the puzzle, bringing the critical missing pieces to the table to create long-term, repeatable, and adaptable processes and successes for every kind of negotiation. It is designed to be a myth-buster, replacing myths and beliefs with practical, clear approaches and structures to ensure that all negotiated outcomes will serve and succeed for the organization. These approaches and structures include the following.

> **Alignment:** While every negotiator in the world pursues "the best deal possible," organizations often have very little definition or clarity on what "best" even means. Alignment between the organization's goals and strategies and the individual negotiator's goals and interests is critical across a number of areas, including:
>
> * Organizational strategy fully aligning with the goals of each negotiation
> * Organizational priorities aligning with the level of support and resources allocated to each negotiation process
> * Individual goals and interests aligning with the organization's goals and strategy
>
> **Measurement:** Any robust system needs good data and information to continuously improve. Negotiation is no different. Metrics that track the organization's processes, goals, and outcomes must be directly connected to what has been achieved in each negotiation to ensure what has been defined as the "best deal" is actually being delivered.
>
> **Skill and Mentoring:** Skill building that is tailored and focused through training, mentoring, and individual needs assessment will help ensure that there is strong institutional memory and support across the negotiation function.
>
> **Customizing:** Tailoring the core negotiation processes to optimize them for each organization will greatly enhance results at the table.
>
> **Creating Institutional Memory:** When negotiation is treated strictly as an individual competency, the skill and knowledge base in

the organization walks out the door every time an employee leaves. By creating strong organizational frameworks, the skill, knowledge and learning from each negotiation and each negotiator is retained and carried forward regularly.

Adapting and Optimizing: Once a strong foundation is built and repeated for each and every negotiation, the organization can turn its attention to optimization, to extending its negotiation skill set to its negotiation partners. By including the other party or parties right from the beginning of every negotiation, outcomes can be achieved that would be impossible as long as each party stays on their side of the fence.

The Negotiation Competent Organization

It should be noted that many people who negotiate for an organization are not professional negotiators by trade. Indeed, many people who conduct important negotiations with outside parties see this as a small, if necessary, side-line activity that takes them away from their important day-to-day job duties. Finance leaders are often arranging payment schedules for suppliers or juggling lines of credit. Operational leaders are often discussing delivery schedules, supply chain parameters, or making decisions on materials and costs. Even salespeople often see their role as simply to sell, not negotiate. This disconnect is a foundational problem for an organization looking to become highly competent in all their negotiations.

Make no mistake, all the aforementioned activities, and many more, are negotiations that affect the success of the organization. The fact that many people who negotiate (as well as the organizations that employ them) do not even consider this work an important and critical activity, a specific skill set that can dramatically improve results, is a leading reason why most negotiations are done in an ad hoc, bordering on random, fashion. For purposes of this book, everyone who discusses and agrees on terms and conditions with outside (or inside) parties is negotiating. The only question is whether they do it well—are they meeting the needs of the organization effectively—or not. To achieve consistently good results, both the individual and the organization need to do their part.

For organizations, this means establishing a clear strategy and direction for the negotiators to follow, investing resources in supporting the negotiation process, and building clear organizational structures and processes that will support and guide each individual toward repeatable success. For individuals, this means understanding the organizational direction and processes and committing to and aligning their behavior to the organizational approach. Negotiators are essentially like commercial airline pilots. Safe and effective pilots, for example, must have strong individual piloting skills. Pilots train and fly hundreds of hours privately before they can be hired as a commercial pilot. Then, they fly hundreds more hours, slowly graduating to larger and larger aircraft. They take simulator training regularly, all to build and maintain their individual skills as pilots.

But looking at the full picture, an airline cannot succeed only by hiring skilled pilots. In addition, they need a full maintenance plan for the planes; they need ground staff to guide the planes to gates; they need navigators, weather monitors, flight data and flight plans that change as conditions change; and they need to be flying to destinations that will be profitable. All of these activities surround the successful pilot; and when the pilot is successful within this complex system, the entire organization is successful as well. Without this interconnected web of supporting activities, a good pilot in an unserviced airplane will either not get off the ground or will crash when trying.

Negotiators, too, need strong systems behind them. They need clear strategic direction, metrics and data, training and mentoring, industry knowledge, and more. And they need alignment between their interests and the organization's interests, as well. Incentives, for example, must be aligned. Paying pilots for how quickly they fly a route would result in planes arriving early and burning far more fuel, clearly not in the organization's interests. In other words, alignment must be in place for pilots and negotiators, for both individual success as well as organizational success.

Behavioral Engineering

In 1978, Thomas F. Gilbert published a landmark book titled *Human Competence: Engineering Worthy Performance*.[10] Gilbert's work focused on ways to build systems that eliminated barriers to both individual and organizational performance. It distinguished between a person's inventory of skills and competencies (what an individual can do on their own) and the environment they operate within (the organizational structures and supports that either enable or impair good results). Gilbert's work is referred to as a "maturity model," a framework to help organizations understand how mature their performance systems currently are, and how well-designed and robust these systems are at any point in time. In essence, Gilbert created a broad, systematic approach to performance, calling it the Behavioral Engineering Model (BEM).

In 2003, Roger Chevalier[11] updated that model based on his own teaching and research. Chevalier also focused very broadly and generically on improving performance in virtually any area of an organization.

It should be clear that the airline industry has followed BEM very successfully. In terms of process, pilots are hired based on their individual skills and experience and trained continuously to ensure they maintain those skills and competencies. Once hired, however, they are embedded in a well-designed, comprehensive environment. Performance for airlines is deliberately engineered, behaviorally engineered, for success. The results are also clear—in spite of how high-risk air travel itself can be, it is the safest means of travel in the world, largely because of the structures that the individuals—pilots in this case—operate within.

The entire negotiation process, something that happens across all organizations, will also benefit from a simple and clear approach that is engineered to deliver success. BEM, however, has never been adapted and applied specifically to the negotiation process.

This book introduces the Negotiation Capability Model (NCM), a further update and refinement of Gilbert and Chevalier's work, which is focused exclusively on engineering repeatable, adaptable, and optimized negotiation performance. Moreover, the NCM is tailored to the needs of specific organizations and negotiators.

Alignment Is Power

This book offers every organization a clear, straightforward process to implement the NCM as a tailored behavioral engineering process into any organization. It will create and sustain alignment between the organization's capabilities and the individual negotiator's capabilities. As the book takes you through the NCM, it will unfold as follows:

Chapter 1: The Negotiation Assessment Tool (NAT). To successfully change and improve any system, a baseline of where we are today must be identified. On any map, whether virtual or paper, the most important point on that map states, "You Are Here." From that reference point, new directions can be taken. The NAT helps every organization assess their starting point based on four simple levels. Once the starting point has been established, the NCM can guide the organization to implement changes and improvements, based on these four levels, as needed in each specific situation.

Chapter 2: Negotiation as Art and Science. Since the NCM has been developed specifically for negotiation performance, the basic principles and approaches to negotiation need to be outlined. In this chapter, an overview of the field of negotiation is given, along with the biases and assumptions that the NCM relies on.

Chapter 3: An Overview of the Negotiation Capability Model (NCM). As a starting point, the four levels of the NCM are outlined and linked to behavioral engineering processes, so leaders can understand how and why the processes and structures this book identifies will lead to dramatically better results. The NCM identifies Level 1: Ad Hockery as the most common state of negotiation practice in most organizations.

Chapter 4: Level 2 NCM—Repeatable Competency. The first step on the journey is to establish a foundation of repeatable processes, skills, and measurements. Without a consistent and clear starting point, all negotiating strategies and skills at the table simply become reactive and ad hoc, leaving outcomes more to chance and luck than anything else.

This chapter gives every organization the framework for creating long-term and repeatable success at the table.

Chapter 5: Level 3 NCM—Adaptive Flexibility. The next step in the NCM, after implementing a foundation of simple and repeatable practices, is freeing up negotiators to become creative, flexible, and adaptable in their negotiation practice, while maintaining and extending the structures put into place at Level 2. Negotiation as an art can succeed only when negotiation as a science has been established as a foundation. Level 3 of the NCM enriches the negotiation process and deepens the skills that can be used at the table, all while remaining in alignment with organizational goals and strategies.

Chapter 6: Level 4 NCM—Optimized Performance. The final step is to extend the negotiation process beyond the limited perspective each party to the deal has, and to practice negotiation as a fully collaborative process, from start to finish. This means engaging the other party from the beginning to jointly create the negotiation process itself. Only by collaborating from the beginning can full value from the relationship be realized.

Chapter 7: Implementing Alignment—Mapping the Journey. How the NCM is implemented makes a difference. In this chapter, two sequences and approaches for putting the NCM into practice will be explored, along with a road map to guide its implementation on any of the three levels.

Chapter 8: Many Forms of Success—The NCM Applied. In this chapter, we will look at a range of different types of negotiations and how the NCM can be applied in a number of different environments.

Chapter 9: Tools and Guides for Assessment, Planning, and Reflection. In this chapter, the book will give the reader practical tools and guides that describe exactly how to assess an organization and how to begin the NCM journey of building and aligning negotiation practices in the organization.

Appendix: A Curated List of Resources. An appendix of resources, with commentary, is included at the end.

Summary

Negotiation has been seen for far too long as a hit-and-miss process based on half the picture—individual skill and success. Too much emphasis has been placed on individual preferences and not the behavioral science that truly drives success. Only when the negotiation process is actually engineered for success, only when the individual's skills and abilities are aligned with and supported by a strong organizational framework, will there be repeatable, adaptable processes that optimize performance at every negotiating table.

Notes

1 Greene, R. (1998). *The 48 laws of power.* Penguin Books.
2 Richard Shell, G. (2018). *Bargaining for advantage: Negotiation strategies for reasonable people.* Penguin Books.
3 Dawson, R. (2006). *Secrets of power salary negotiations.* Career Press.
4 Rosen, D. (2016). *99 negotiating strategies: Tips, tactics & techniques used by Wall Street's toughest dealmakers.* Ross & Rubin Publishers.
5 Voss, C. (2017). *Never split the difference: Negotiating as if your life depended on it.* Random House Business Books.
6 Cohen, H. (1982). *You can negotiate anything.* Bantam.
7 Lawrence, S. (2014). *Good for you, great for me.* PublicAffairs Books.
8 Pfau, B., Kay, I., Murphy, J., & Kilduff, C. (2002). Playing the training game and losing. *HR Magazine,* 47(8), 48.
9 Carnegie Mellon University Software Engineering Institute, The Capability Maturity Model: Guidelines for Improving the Software Process, Addison-Wesley. (1999). Dave Melton & Peter Van Dyne, Don't get caught in the training trap. *Transport Topics,* 3631, 7 (2005).
10 Gilbert, T. F. (2007). *Human competence: Engineering worthy behavior.* Pfeiffer.
11 https://onlinelibrary.wiley.com/doi/abs/10.1002/pfi.4930420504

1   The Negotiation Assessment Tool

Imagine, for a moment, a heart surgeon. A patient arrives complaining of chest pain. The surgeon leaps into action, immediately performing a quadruple bypass on the patient, only to find the patient was suffering from poorly digested tacos, not a heart condition. We would easily call this malpractice, since every professional in the world is expected to diagnose first, to assess the issue or problem before starting to try and fix that problem. For example, how many of us would allow a mechanic to replace the engine in our car simply because it wouldn't start? We would likely insist on finding out what the problem is first—and only then decide what to do about it. Assessing and understanding a problem is the critical first step in most situations.

Good quality diagnostic tools and information are required for proper assessment. We expect doctors to diagnose using the proper equipment, such as MRI and blood tests. We expect auto mechanics to diagnose problems with pressure gauges, electrical meters, and now computer diagnostics. For effective negotiations, we need to diagnose the problems and assess the outcomes to understand what creates and maintains success for the organization. For something as mundane as our car, we have a dashboard of information and a handful of warning lights to tell us how the car is operating every time we drive it. When something needs attention, such as air in the tires or an oil change, the car's system lets us know. Yet how many organizations have a dashboard or warning lights to alert them to the fact that their negotiation processes need attention? That they will not get us to our destination?

In reality, many organizations and many negotiators lack good data and metrics; they rarely have well-defined goals and objectives; and most have never held post-negotiation reviews as a way to learn and improve. Most feedback relies on either the subjective reporting of the negotiator—"It was tough, but we did the best we could,"—or on assessing the narrowest terms of the contract—price, for example— to decide whether the negotiation was successful. In other words, the organization has no frame of reference for understanding the negotiation process and few ways to assess whether the results were actually as

DOI:10.4324/9781003243854-2

good as they could have been or have met the most important needs of the organization.

This leads most organizations back to that most dangerous myth of negotiations—that negotiation is an individual activity, that negotiations succeed or fail based on the skill and ability of one, or even a few, individuals at the table. Individual negotiation skills, as we've said, are important, but are nowhere near enough to ensure success on a regular basis. We put our faith in the person leading the negotiations and hope they deliver a good result each and every time. And if they don't, we blame that individual and replace them.

As one wag once put it, changing negotiators when they fail is a lot like changing deck chairs on the Titanic—regardless of where you're sitting, the ship is still going down. Until the organization can identify where negotiations fail and why they succeed, until they can navigate those difficult waters, they will be prone to hitting icebergs rather regularly. And like the iceberg that the Titanic hit, the choice of negotiator is really just the tip of that iceberg. What lies below the water, out of sight, is what creates success, what supports the tip of the iceberg that we actually see.

What supports success in any negotiation are two critical elements that rarely get the attention they deserve. First, the clarity of the strategy, values, goals, and interests that essentially define what success actually means. And second, how well the frameworks, processes, measurements, resources, and incentives within the organization are aligned to develop, support, and guide the negotiators at the table toward that success. In this chapter, we will see how to assess the current level of effectiveness of any organization's structures and processes in their negotiation function. The result of this assessment will help to create a clear path to consistently better outcomes, a plan for implementing simple structures and processes so that negotiation becomes a competitive advantage in meeting the organization's strategic goals.

Negotiation Assessment Tool (NAT)

The first step in dramatically improving negotiated outcomes is diagnosing and assessing the current state of affairs. A common view from the medical world puts it simply: "Prescription without diagnosis is malpractice." We agree. The first step toward engineering better performance through the Negotiation Capability Model (NCM) is having a simple diagnostic tool for understanding the status quo, for understanding what is being done well and what is missing. The NAT does this.

The NAT identifies four distinct levels of the NCM and identifies how effectively any given organization is approaching their negotiation process. Each level has clear behavioral markers that can be easily recognized and assessed.

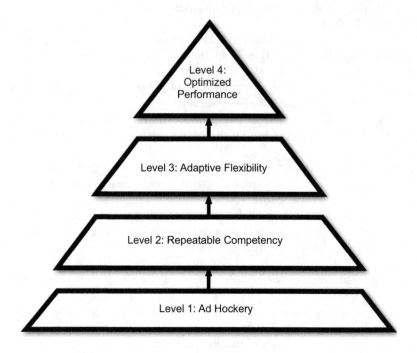

Figure 1.1 The Negotiation Assessment Tool

Level 1: Ad Hockery

Few organizations pay zero attention to how they negotiate important matters. Most commonly, however, negotiations are led by busy people who tend to prepare just before they go to the table. They cram in whatever prework and preparation they can given their time pressures and resources. Each negotiation gets time and attention at the last minute, and negotiations take place in a fluid, shifting environment, a type of "just in time" negotiation. Each negotiation looks different from the last, each is prepared for on a one-off basis, reactively rather than proactively. Unfortunately, anything done from a seat-of-the-pants reactive perspective is not a failed system. It is no system at all. It is an approach we call Ad Hockery.

Ad Hockery is the most common state of negotiations for many organizations. The business environment is constantly shifting—other parts of the organization are grappling with different challenges; priorities either change or are subject to competing interests within the organization; people come and go—and in the middle of all this we have to negotiate a supplier contract, a collective agreement, a strategic partnership, venture capital financing, a distribution agreement, and so on. The organization, not knowing what else to do, hands this off to its top negotiator in the organization, who jumps in at the eleventh hour. Or the organization presumes that someone

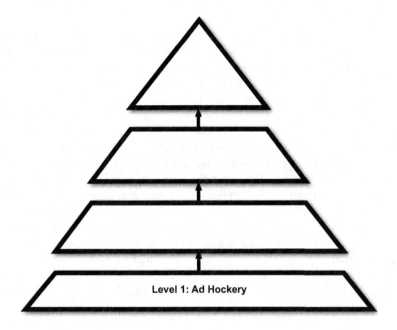

Figure 1.2 Ad Hockery

with professional expertise or significant knowledge of the situation will also be an effective negotiator, regardless of their understanding or experience of negotiation as its own area of competence. There is a belief that simply being articulate and knowledgeable will be enough for success at the negotiation table. And everyone, in the end, does the best they can.

Under these circumstances, each and every negotiation, each and every outcome, ends up being unique. And ad hoc. Ad Hockery looks something like this:

- Negotiation is the responsibility of each individual who negotiates. They are accountable for delivering a deal, and only the deal itself is assessed in the end. Some in the organization like it, some don't. We move on.
- Negotiation processes vary widely—no systematic or standard approach exists, each negotiator does what makes sense to them—some prepare weeks in advance, some the night before.
- Negotiators rely heavily on tactics they've learned about through trial and error, or tips and tricks they learned in a short training course they took a few years ago.
- Negotiations are high-stakes, often driven by a predictable deadline but left to the last minute (a contract expiring, a sudden change in costs).
- Negotiations are high on adrenaline, brinkmanship, and luck; they are low on planning.

- Few measurements or metrics guide the system—anecdotal information is the best available data.
- Each negotiation is conducted within its own context (often resembling a vacuum). The broader organizational strategy and values are rarely included in the process; or worse they are seen as the exclusive purview of senior management and simply not shared or communicated.
- Negotiators are either hired for their experience or are offered a few days of training at a generic training program. This training, if offered, is rarely linked to the organization's specific needs, strategies, or values.
- The "best" deal is achieved, whatever that means at the time, and the organization adapts to it and moves on to the next challenge.
- Negotiation success depends only on moves made at the bargaining table in real time. There is very little thought given to the broader negotiation process itself.
- Negotiations typically focus on numbers and highly "tangible" elements of the deal, with both sides often jumping into trading offers quite early in the process. Many deals are achieved through "horse-trading" at the end of the day.
- Negotiations often feel quite difficult, and idioms such as, "We knew it was the best deal possible because we were equally unhappy," characterize the thinking.

Organizations stuck in Ad Hockery are truly stuck. Without a foundation or a baseline approach that is understood and applied, the random effects of Ad Hockery will simply continue. Combined with the fact that the odd negotiation exceeds the organization's expectations, it can even appear that this ad hoc approach works—like the gambler who remembers only the few hands they won, forgetting or ignoring all the losses that came before and after that rare winning hand. Unfortunately, at least some of the time we feel like we won. Other times, we're not sure if we succeeded or not, to be honest. We may walk away thinking we achieved something when there was actually a much more advantageous deal to be made.

A recent client is a good example. A manufacturer and its union typically negotiated a collective agreement every two to three years. On the union side, the team had about 80% turnover on their bargaining team each time they negotiated. On the management side, they had lower turnover on their bargaining team, but senior management did change regularly, and the organization seemed to alternate between having the director of labor relations lead the team and hiring an outside negotiator to come in and lead the bargaining for them.

In every round of bargaining, either one side or the other had new leadership and each round of bargaining was different. The parties rarely spoke before arriving at the table, and each round had major surprises that often stalled negotiations, sometimes for weeks, even months. Because of this history, management rarely shared all their information with the union, fearing it would be used against them. Both parties relied on cherry-picked information taken from various sources, such as the current rate of inflation or the current unemployment rate, with very little context. Without good processes and clear information, bargaining each round turned into a simple test of wills. Over many years, few changes to the collective agreement were negotiated by the parties unless an actual strike or lockout took place. Neither party could predict what would happen at the table, and both accepted deals they didn't like, only because it was better than another labor disruption. Ad Hockery reigned for many years before the parties started to think that there might be a better way. That better way is establishing repeatable competency in the negotiation process.

Level 2: Repeatable Competency

Level 2 of the NCM is the level of Repeatable Competency and is the starting point for building a negotiation system that will deliver consistently good outcomes for the organization. Repeatability is the foundation for being able to sustain success. It's only when we have a consistent approach, however simple, that we can start to identify what activities promote success, what kind of preparation helps build agreements that meet the parties' needs, and what behaviors strengthen the relationship with the other party. Having a repeatable negotiation process is the first level where there is actually a "system" in place. Without a system of some kind, Ad Hockery is the order of the day—every negotiation is different and each negotiation comes with unexpected surprises that cause both parties to react reflexively under pressure.

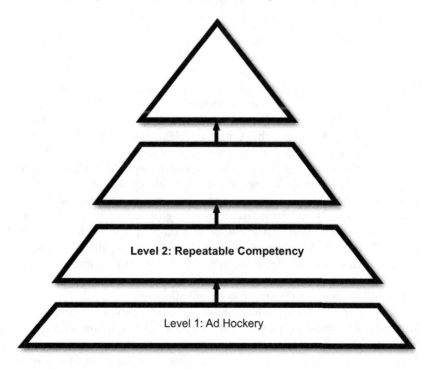

Figure 1.3 Repeatable Competency

When an organization has a repeatable process built on basic competencies, the focus is primarily internal. The basics are given the attention they deserve. Level 2 creates and supports some of the following:

- An understanding of the role the organization itself plays in ensuring repeatable successes in key negotiations
- Clarity of organizational strategy, values, and direction that can be used to support individual negotiators
- A process for preparation that is enacted well in advance of a negotiation, with enough time to do it well. Preparation can include some or all of the following:
  o Understanding what happened in prior negotiations
  o Collecting clear data and metrics within the organization
  o Completing a needs analysis with internal stakeholders
  o Aligning organizational goals and values with individual negotiator behaviors
  o Training negotiators in the appropriate negotiation skills and behaviors
  o Giving individual negotiators access to peers and mentors for support
  o Creating a strategy for each negotiation that defines success, along with an understanding of why
  o Developing a clear communication and feedback process to monitor the negotiation as it proceeds in real time

A basic repeatable approach serves as the price of admission into the world of professional negotiation practices that yield consistent results. Level 2 organizations have a clear framework along with repeatable processes that help the organization quickly discover what activities lead to stronger preparation, better outcomes, and more effective strategies when negotiating.

Tired of Ad Hockery on their sales team, a new sales manager introduced new activities and required them from all salespeople. First, they required that salespeople not meet with clients until they had a history on both the prospect and the person they would be negotiating with. Second, they asked for a description of their strategy in meeting with a prospect—what information the salesperson wanted to gather before any presentation, a clear needs analysis from the client, and a specific goal for the first and second meeting with each client. They insisted that the first meeting not have the goal of closing a deal—that could come only in the second meeting. Finally, they required that each salesperson talk to their production staff internally for volume and delivery time estimates before any second meeting, to ensure they could manage the clients' expectations effectively.

The result was an improved ratio of time spent negotiating to deals made—their salespeople spent far less time with prospects that simply weren't going to be good clients. In addition, client satisfaction also went up, helping improve the retention rate for renewals. Since managing client expectations was now built in as part of the sales process, these metrics started to improve across the board. Finally, a client feedback process they introduced showed that clients were impressed—salespeople had a good background on them and clearly understood their business needs better than their competitors. In addition, they felt they could trust the company more, a key indicator of long-term success.

Level 3: Adaptive Flexibility

After an organization has focused internally and implemented consistent processes and a framework that all negotiations follow, the negotiators can then start to focus more of their attention across the table in their preparation. Level 3 of the NCM brings a focus on adapting the repeatable processes implemented at Level 2, adding skills and strategies specific to each negotiation. When there is a deeper focus across the table during preparation, it becomes easier to modify negotiation strategies during the negotiation itself. In this way, adaptability and flexibility become core competencies. The negotiation system can become more tailored and more nuanced to respond to unique situations with unique solutions that can benefit both parties.

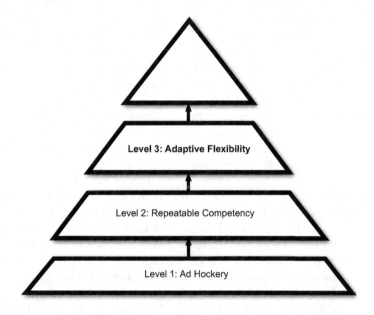

Figure 1.4 Adaptable Flexibility

Level 3 focuses on the following processes:

- Deeper use of metrics in guiding negotiations, especially metrics that focus on data and information about the party across the table
- Deeper use of negotiating skills in the preparation phase. This might include analysis and application of important negotiating tools such as Best Alternative to No Agreement (BATNA) and Worst Alternative to

No Agreement (WATNA), assessment of the negotiating styles of the other party, and so on
- Better research on the other parties' history, needs, values, and interests before any negotiation takes place
- Setting clear relationship goals as part of the negotiation process
- Ongoing assessment processes to identify when to step back and adjust mid-negotiation, if needed
- In-depth debrief of every negotiation to enable a continuous learning process for the whole organization

A large chemical plant and refinery was owned by three joint venture partner corporations, each one owning a different percentage of the facility. They had struck a joint venture council where issues and concerns were brought. Over the years, this council became less and less effective. The largest partner, a major oil company, owned 45%, and felt that the partnership was struggling. Each party had noticeable turnover in their senior leadership, and the newer members of each team resisted the way the council raised and addressed issues. There was a great deal of back-channel talk, little progress on the larger issues, and the partnership was clearly strained. The council had clear (if rigid) protocols for creating agendas, deciding which issues would be addressed, how often they met, and who would attend. But it wasn't working.

The largest partner finally put their concerns on the table, along with a proposal to revamp the council's negotiation and problem-solving processes at a basic level. To their surprise, the other two partners quickly agreed. They discovered that the basic framework for the partnership was still working but simply wasn't flexible or creative enough to address the problems they were facing. With the help of an outside facilitator, barriers were identified, better measurements were put in place to monitor the speed and focus of issues that were raised, different types of issues (technical, human resource, marketing/sales, etc.) were categorized along with different approaches that were tailored to each type of problem. Parties began speaking frankly at council meetings instead of after the meeting, leading to a far better understanding of each other's goals and objectives. As speed-to-solution improved dramatically, best practices began to be shared and tried in different areas of the partnership. All partners reported a significant improvement in alignment and collaboration at the facility.

Where Level 2 establishes a basic system focused internally, Level 3 extends that internal system to include a clearer focus on understanding the other party and the relationship, creating critical intelligence to help the negotiator engage and problem-solve effectively at the table. In addition, continuous learning becomes automatic, turning the negotiation experience into a learning center for the whole organization.

Level 4: Optimized Performance

In Level 3, some focus on the other party, on their values, needs and interests, takes place. Level 4 of the NCM, however, turns each negotiation into a form of partnership, one where value gains are made jointly. The process starts by engaging the other party to jointly build the negotiation process. Rather than each party preparing separately and meeting at the table, parties meet early and prepare the process from the beginning, often designing joint data collection and sharing, engaging subject matter experts, and identifying mutual value gains together. It is only after Level 3 is strong and adaptable that Level 4 can be reached.

Figure 1.5 Optimized Performance

Level 4 processes can include the following:

- Negotiation strategies and goals are shared at the beginning of the process, and negotiations aim to transparently maximize both parties' interests
- Parties prioritize the relationship as a core value in the negotiation
- Effective use of negotiation aids, such as software systems and joint data gathering, allow for deep data creation and sharing
- Negotiations take a medium- to long-term view from both parties' perspective
- Value creation takes a significantly larger role than value claiming
- Negotiation strategies are adopted that may impact the norms and standards of the industry itself

Level 4 is not achieved often, for a couple of reasons. First, and most likely, is that few parties achieve Level 3 adaptability and flexibility in their negotiation practices. Level 3 requires resources, focus, and leadership to achieve, and frequently Level 2 is seen as a significant enough accomplishment. Level

3 requires full organizational alignment to ensure that negotiation successes are not simply the result of Ad Hockery and luck, not the result of one talented individual who may or may not stay with the organization for the long term or who may not be able to repeat their success.

Second, Level 4 requires the right situation and context. Some negotiations are strategically more transactional and not intended to be long term. In these situations, Level 3 capability is the end point, the level that will bring maximum value to that type of negotiation.

In the area of mergers and acquisitions, for example, Level 4 negotiation approaches can be critical to creating and sustaining value. According to *Forbes* magazine,[1] between 70% and 90% of mergers and acquisitions fail to provide any value—an astonishing statistic. This failure rate is attributed, in part, to an unclear or absent social compact between leadership teams. In other words, the leadership teams didn't engage in negotiating the process together, from the start, the way these two organizations did:

> Company A made a bid to purchase Company B. Company B produced a specialized product and was also known for having a unique, flat organizational structure and culture that was a key to its success. Rather than approach the purchase as a takeover, Company A met with senior leadership at B and proposed more of a "merger of equals" approach. Together, they identified metrics for success, jointly agreed specific areas where B's management team would have sole or primary decision-making, and jointly agreed on a five-year strategic plan for the merged entities. Then the parties agreed on a new organizational chart for B, along with leadership attributes for any new leaders being recruited to ensure there was a cultural fit for B's values. Only then did A and B negotiate a price and share swap structure that met both parties' needs.

NAT Questionnaire

Once the NAT's four levels are clear and understood, the first step for every organization is to assess the current level of practice within their organization. Each organization needs to know its starting point, what practices are or are not in place, before any plans to make changes are considered. The NAT questionnaire is the starting point.

Designed as a simple evaluative tool, the NAT questionnaire will identify where an organization currently exists on the NCM, whether an ad hoc approach is prevalent, where there are activities that are repeatable and consistent, where practices go beyond repeatable to adaptable, and where the organization has actually optimized the negotiation process. This questionnaire can be used to evaluate the organization as a whole or assess specific areas within the organization, as needed.

In addition, the NAT questionnaire assesses practices across three broad organizational areas, categories that will be targeted for improvement through the NCM framework which will be introduced in Chapter 3.

Figure 1.6 Three Organizational Capabilities

These areas include the following:

- **Strategy, Values, and Direction**: How clearly and effectively is the strategy of the organization built into and reflected in all negotiation activities? What organizational values have been embedded in the process? How has the organization prioritized negotiation as a critical success factor?
- **Human Capital and Organizational Investment:** How has the organization invested in and supported the negotiation function? What approach to hiring the right people and retaining negotiation staff is in place? How clear are the expectations, roles, and responsibilities for both negotiation staff and support staff?
- **Organizational Incentives:** How well designed are the incentives, both monetary and nonmonetary, around the negotiation function? What is incentivized, and how does that affect negotiation outcomes?

A basic version of the NAT questionnaire is given in Chapter 9.

The NAT Questionnaire Applied

To get a practical sense of the value of assessing where on the NCM an organization is performing, the following are two examples from organizations that have applied the NAT, one a nonprofit and the other a manufacturer.

Organization #1: The ABC Foundation is a nonprofit that receives government funding for basic operational expenses and fundraises for the additional money it uses to run programs for disabled people. Their fundraising staff is constantly negotiating with wealthy individuals for large legacy donations, looking for donation amounts, timetables, and opportunities to name programs or endowments after the individuals or families giving significant gifts. ABC has not been seeing increases in their donation base from higher-end wealthy philanthropists as they would like to. The organization conducted a negotiation assessment using the NAT, which revealed the following.

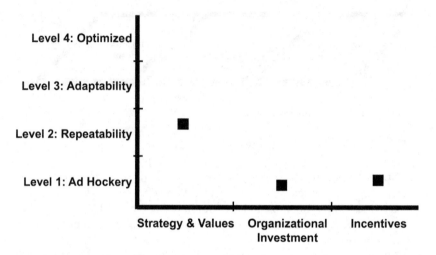

Figure 1.7 NAT Results for ABC Foundation

As you can see from the NAT for ABC Foundation, the organization functions reasonably well at Level 2 on the strategy side, in that it pays attention to its strategy, values, and goals in most of its negotiations. It conveys the overall goals and values both to its negotiation staff as well as to its donors. When it comes to investing resources in hiring, training, and supporting its negotiation staff, it operates only on an ad hoc basis, basically letting their staff fend for themselves. On the incentives side, they experience frustration and turnover since negotiation staff do not see a long-term future or career path within the organization. In both the latter areas, the organization is solidly in Ad Hockery, which is fully reflected in the outcomes and results they are seeing.

Organization #2: The XYZ Corporation manufactures circuit boards mainly used in smart appliances. They have been struggling with bursts of strong growth followed by periods of flat sales for the last five years. They have had a medium level of turnover in sales staff that they don't understand, since they offer one of the highest commission packages in the industry and spend significant money on high-level training and support for the sales team. The organization conducted a negotiation assessment with the NAT, with the following results.

The NAT chart for XYZ Corp. let them see two causes for their mediocre results. First, their strategy is solidly in Ad Hockery, meaning that there is very poorly sustained direction and focus at the strategic level for the

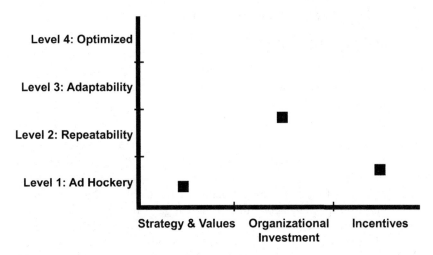

Figure 1.8 NAT Results for XYZ Corp.

salespeople—they simply don't see a bigger picture they can get behind. In addition, even though significant focus has been put on training and support for the sales team, and even though commissions on the incentive side are high, there is very little alignment between these three areas. This has, ironically, reduced the level of commitment and value for the investment XYZ has made in their human capital and incentive program.

Summary

The starting point for every organization is effectively assessing their current practices. This will identify practices that can remain and be strengthened, as well as identifying key gaps where the approach is more random and ad hoc, typically costing the organization significantly in outcomes.

After a clear assessment of an organization's negotiation capability using tools such as the NAT questionnaire, what is needed next is a comprehensive understanding of this: What negotiation processes—what specific activities and best practices—can be identified and implemented to raise the whole organization into Level 2 and beyond? The NCM provides the framework to answer this question across six critical areas and helps create alignment from the organizational level right down to the individual negotiator level.

Before we get there, however, an understanding of the negotiation field and its underlying values and assumptions is necessary.

Note

1 www.forbes.com/sites/forbescoachescouncil/2019/06/24/most-mergers-fail-because-people-arent-boxes/?sh=6e50ee2d5277

2 Negotiation as Art and Science

The negotiation field has spawned many different philosophies and ideas, everything from power negotiating to mutual gains bargaining, from win/win to win/lose, from competitive to cooperative to collaborative, and everything in between. The field has also promoted a wide range of strategies, tactics, attitudes, and behaviors, many of which are contradictory—be strong, be collaborative, make the first offer, never make the first offer, keep them off-balance, be nice, tell a good story, show flexibility, never compromise, knowledge is power, never share more information than you need to. And so on.

These many different terminologies and styles have only served to clutter the field, often obscuring the fact that negotiating, at its core, is simple. Negotiation, in reality, is a form of problem-solving, and whether a problem is large or small, it can be broken down into a series of simple concepts that rely on a small number of equally simple tools and skills. This simplicity, however, does not make it easy to master, and it does not minimize what can be achieved through the negotiation process. The tools used to build the ancient pyramids were also seemingly simple—the ancient Egyptians had none of the complex and impressive machinery we have today. Yet these colossal structures built using basic concepts and tools are still some of the most impressive in the world.

In part, the reason the pyramids are still standing today is that even thousands of years ago the pyramid builders understood that it's the strength of the foundation—whether for a pyramid, a house, or an organization—that will determine success. The same holds true for a process like negotiating. The foundational principles and processes, if strong, will lead to long-term success.

Once a strong foundation is in place, once there is a common understanding and framework for practicing negotiation, individual negotiators can flourish, can begin to apply creative and flexible skills and approaches that take the negotiation process into the realm of art. Without a strong foundation in place, however, negotiation reverts quickly to Ad Hockery.

In this chapter, we will identify the foundational principles, ideas, and tools that long-term negotiation success rests on. These tools are basic and simple. And necessary.

DOI:10.4324/9781003243854-3

The Foundations of Negotiation

The field of negotiation, in many ways, was defined and professionalized in 1965 by Walton and McKersie's *A Behavioural Theory of Labor Negotiations*.[1] Walton and McKersie created the groundwork for the first structured approach to understanding negotiation, and to understanding and categorizing the wide range of behaviors that occurred at the bargaining table. Negotiation then entered the mainstream in 1981 with Roger Fisher and William Ury's book *Getting to Yes*.[2] Fisher and Ury built on Walton and McKersie's work by broadening it from its narrow focus on labor negotiations to creating a framework that any type of negotiation could be understood and assessed through. These seminal works contributed to a deeper understanding of the key dynamics in negotiations and how individuals tend to behave. Concepts such as positional versus mutual gains bargaining, win-win versus win-lose negotiation, common versus competing interests, and early thoughts on recognizing the value and importance of the preparation process for negotiations advanced the science of negotiation immeasurably.

What Fisher and Ury as well as Walton and McKersie looked at was the idea of how parties saw, or framed, negotiation as a process.

Negotiation Frames

What is your mental frame for negotiation? How does your organization think of negotiation and what imagery and language does it follow? Is there a clear right or wrong framing that we should all adopt? Does it matter? These authors, and many others, saw that how we frame or understand the negotiation process deeply influences our behavior as we negotiate. And by extension, the results we achieve.

Is negotiation seen as just a big poker match? A game where we constantly try to see who has the best hand and determine when someone is merely bluffing? Or is it a game of tennis, volleying back and forth and trying to keep your opponent off-balance until the timing is right to go for the kill shot? Is it war, where we assemble an arsenal and use this strength to impose our will upon others? Is it Shakespeare, a theatrical endeavor with a new language and a mix of drama and comedy? Is it a math problem like an equation that can be solved with a clear right or wrong answer? Is it dancing, a learnable set of moves done together that must sync up to the music of the moment? Is it baking where all we need to do is bake a bigger pie and everyone will enjoy a larger slice of dessert? Is it art or is it science?

The point of these questions is to help us assess how our organization and our staff see and run the negotiation process. How many different conceptions of negotiation exist within the organization? How clearly aligned (or misaligned) is each person's understanding of negotiation? How did this mindset come to be, and should it change?

Walton and McKersie were the first to challenge the normal framing of negotiation as a competitive sport. Fisher and Ury took it much further, revolutionizing the thinking and the approach to negotiation worldwide. They both achieved this by identifying one of the most foundational ideas in negotiation—the difference between distributive versus integrative bargaining.[3]

Distributive Versus Integrative

As humans, we are quite predisposed to seeing the world through a lens of scarcity, which leads us to believe quite strongly that what we want or need must be at the expense of others. In negotiation, where interdependence is part of the activity itself, we so often view our path to gaining what we need (winning) as one that requires others to give up what they need (losing). In other words, we see the process as simply there to distribute what is being negotiated—money, products, goods or services, and so on. This zero-sum distributive mindset, this idea that what I gain must be a loss for you, is deeply embedded in human culture through the idea of competition. Since the beginning of time, competition has been linked to survival. People and animals compete for food, for status, for money. On top of that, many of the great pleasures in life are competitive—sports, school grades, and even work promotions—and all seem to enshrine competition as the framework the whole human process operates within. When Darwin published his seminal theory of evolution, it was founded on natural selection or survival of the fittest. All life was seen as a competition where only the winners survived. Distributive negotiation mirrors this competitive and "win-lose" approach to bargaining.

Take, for example, sports. All sports are designed to have winners and losers, with the critical determinant of success being whether or not we scored just a bit more than our opponent. Even the definition of the word "compete" has evolved over the years to embrace a zero-sum mindset. While originally meaning "to strive in common" or "to come together, agree," the meaning of competition has shifted as our own presumptions have evolved, to mean that we are "in rivalry against someone else."[4] In the capitalist marketplace, this zero-sum mentality has been deeply reinforced with antitrust laws that send the message that competition is king, and collaboration is seen as both unethical and illegal—ignoring the fact that negotiation and collaboration underpin just about everything inside and outside every organization, and that only narrow types of collusion outside the organization are barred.

Overcoming this distributive, zero-sum mindset is no easy task. While individual negotiators often realize the limitations of a win-lose mindset and move toward a more "win-win" approach, this often puts the individual out of alignment with the organizational mindset and culture where winning is simply expected. It is, in fact, the organization that needs to lead this change. We argue that it is a core cultural item for organizations to better understand and embrace the effectiveness of a more integrative, a more win-win framing of virtually all negotiation situations.

What is not often realized is that win-win and win-lose are not the only results of any given negotiation or competition. A third outcome, a "lose-lose" outcome, is often ignored by the parties, only to their detriment. In fact, when parties compete, they often assume that, like the many sports we love to watch, the only thing to be decided is which team will win. It seems obvious that when one team loses, the other must win. In our work and personal lives, however, lose-lose outcomes are a very real possibility, a direct result of seeing and approaching the negotiation process as a way to decide which side wins.

Take civil litigation. When parties sue each other, it seems pretty clear that each side believes that when they win, the money to make it all worthwhile will automatically follow. In truth, this is rarely the case. A civil justice review in the province of Ontario, Canada,[5] for example, demonstrated the folly of this belief. The average judgment awarded to a plaintiff in the civil courts in the 1990s was approximately $58,000. Yet the typical cost *per party* (for a three-day trial, considered quite short) was close to $60,000. This meant that, together, the parties were spending close to $120,000 on a system that awarded a winning party (and assuming that they won!) only $58,000[6] against a cost of $60,000. Many times, the award was far less than the claim, as well. It's true that the winning party could also be awarded some of their legal costs, but this was rarely more than 40–50% of their actual costs. A typical result had the "winner" awarded $20,000 of their claimed $58,000, spending $60,000 and getting costs awarded of $25,000. The net result, *for the winner*, was a loss of $15,000. The "loser" in this case lost even more: $20,000 on the claim, $25,000 in costs to the winner plus the $60,000 they spent on their own lawyer, for a total loss of over $100,000. In other words, most civil litigation claims are much more likely to be lose-lose for both parties, much more likely that both parties will be worse off in the end than any other outcome. The relentless pursuit of winning is the single biggest reason for lose-lose outcomes.

A more integrative approach—a problem-solving mindset where interests are pursued without assuming others need to lose something for you to achieve them—is a foundational concept that both individuals and organizations need to understand and structurally support to be successful in key negotiations. Integrative negotiation focuses on finding creative solutions that don't require either party to achieve their goals at the other party's expense. While win-win has become somewhat popularized as an easy shortcut for challenging a zero-sum mindset, in reality it takes determination and skill to achieve one's own interests without simply taking it from the other party. In fact, integrative bargaining demands not only that you achieve what you need, it also demands that the other party also get their needs met as well. This requires a focus and skill set quite different than simply competing with each other at the bargaining table.

Even in the world of economics, a field founded on the concept of competition, the idea of distributive negotiating where one party's gain must be at another party's expense is no longer accepted wisdom. As James Heckman, the 2000 Nobel laureate in economics said, "The single biggest misunderstanding built into the mentality of popular culture is that one person's gain is another person's loss." Successful negotiation, in other words, can almost always result in both parties gaining value.

The challenge, however, is that most organizations are structured and individuals are incentivized to pursue zero-sum strategies and distributive tactics, even when they may believe there is a more productive, a more integrative, approach. This book provides clear strategies for how to overcome this foundational barrier.

So, Just Be Cooperative?

So, if it's just as simple as getting rid of our win-lose mindset, does that mean if we simply cooperate with the other side during negotiations all will be well? To answer this, let's talk about a classic negotiation game.

"Win As Much As You Can"[7] is an important negotiation game examining this tension between cooperation and competition. It is typically a ten-round negotiation game between four individuals (or organizations) where the goal is to maximize one's own score. For each round, participants have two basic choices, play an X or play a Y, and the score is determined by the combination of your own choice combined with the choices of your three negotiation counterparts.

After each round, the combinations of Xs and Ys are recorded, and each team receives points based on how many players played each card, the X or the Y. As you can see from the payoff schedule in Figure 2.1, playing the X card is linked to being competitive and self-interested, and playing the Y card is linked to being cooperative, as follows:

Payoff Schedule	
4 Xs:	Lose 1 each
3 Xs:	Win 1 each
1 Y:	Lose 3
2 Xs:	Win 2 each
2 Ys:	Lose 2 each
1 X:	Win 3
3 Ys:	Lose 1 each
4 Ys:	Win 1 each

Figure 2.1 Prisoner's Dilemma Payoff Schedule

This is a classic Prisoner's Dilemma[8] game designed to explore how each player can best maximize their own self-interest—how to gain the most points. This seemingly simple game has many nuanced sub-lessons around negotiation, but at its core it is exploring this choice around cooperation and whether cooperation or competition will result in win–win, win–lose, lose–win, or lose–lose outcomes.

For example, one party trying an "Always Cooperate" strategy of playing all Ys may seem to make sense but typically fails when the other parties simply take advantage of the constant Y being played. As an aggressive union negotiator once said, "If I kick you in the teeth and you keep giving me what I want, ask yourself—why would I change?" A purely competitive strategy of always playing Xs would seem to maximize your own scoring but only if everyone else consistently keeps playing Ys. But why would they do that? How many negotiators, charged with their own individual or organizational targets, would be willing to continue taking it on the chin as the other party wins? Not many. Because of this, the game often results in all parties playing X, and all parties losing, over and over. Of course, there are many strategies between always cooperating and never cooperating. So what strategy leads to the greatest amount of success, leading to the highest scores?

In the late 1970s, a number of computer tournaments were held to answer exactly this question—which negotiation strategy optimizes our own success?[9] Those initial tournaments consistently found that a simple strategy of "Tit For Tat," starting with cooperation and then mirroring whatever your negotiation counterpart did in the previous round, was highly successful. This "an eye for an eye but a gift for a gift" was a pretty good strategy for finding this balance between cooperation and competition. This was updated a bit with a strategy called "Win-Stay, Lose-Shift", that built off of the Tit For Tat principles of starting cooperative with a Y, punishing pure competitors by matching their X so they lose rather than win, and also taking full advantage of those who blindly continue cooperating regardless of losing. The primary point is this: we must be prepared to adapt to the circumstances to avoid a quick devolution into ongoing lose–lose outcomes. Even where our primary goal is our own "win," we must be attuned to the idea that a more collaborative, problem-solving stance is far more likely to get us there. A winning strategy is far more nuanced than blindly cooperating or blindly competing.

This idea that purely competitive or purely cooperative positions are often predisposed to failure is a monumental shift for many individual negotiators. We need to seek something different, a flexibly collaborative mindset, one that can understand the complexities at play in our negotiations, creatively explore interests and the dynamics of the moment, and respond appropriately when another party becomes competitive. At the organizational level, this shift is transformational.

Interests

A young girl hurriedly walks toward the final box of Cracker Jack[10] located at the long end of the snack aisle. Just as she arrives and reaches for the box, a teenage boy appears to suddenly grab part of the box and declares it as his own. Both hold on to the one box tightly and begin to argue over who is the rightful owner. The girl pleads, "I saw it first!" The boy retorts, "I called ahead to make sure the store still had a box left!" The fight continues to escalate, each making claims and justifications, each insisting they are clearly in the right. So, what should they do to resolve this heated negotiation that has only just begun to escalate?

Perhaps they could bring in a third-party, like the store clerk, to decide who can buy it. Maybe they can look at the facts of the case, such as who first had possession of the box? Did the boy actually call the store, were they holding the item for him? Who saw it first, or who touched it first? Or maybe the older boy can simply overpower the young girl? How about a coin flip, or a battle of wits with the age-old game of rock/paper/scissors (lizard/Spock)?[11] A wrestling match might seemingly favor the teenage boy but bigger upsets in sport have occurred. Maybe a compromise is in order, and they should simply split the cost of the box and divide everything in half?

What is the ideal way to resolve a negotiation entrenched in the opposing positions of "I want it!" and "No! I want it!"? As happens often in negotiation, everyone focuses so heavily on their own desired outcomes or positions that they fail to ask the underlying question of, "Why do you want what you want?" Perhaps, if we explored the why behind this simple, yet passionate, negotiation we might learn the following: the teenage boy has been collecting the toys inside Cracker Jack boxes since he was three years old and is hoping that a rare toy he needs to complete his collection is in this very box. Furthermore, we might learn that he is allergic to peanuts (yes, a dangerous condition for someone collecting Cracker Jack toys!) and doesn't touch the delicious snack inside. As we turn to the girl to ask her why she wants the box, we might learn that she has been craving the caramel popcorn and nuts in Cracker Jack for weeks before finally locating a box. A shipping problem had made them nearly impossible to find. Probing more, we might also learn that she thinks the prizes are silly and throws them away, rarely even opening the small toy in the first place. Armed with this new information, even the most novice negotiator can now see a solution where they each get what they really want—a snack for one and a toy for the other—without compromise and without escalation.

In case this example feels too simple or contrived to apply anywhere else, how hard is it to imagine a patent dispute being resolved with one party commercializing the patent in the medical imaging industry and the other party applying it in the security screening field, for example?

Interests, uncovering the *why* behind all the potential positions or demands that might be presented, are the fundamental currency for organizations to be successful at problem-solving through integrative negotiation. When we understand the why, like in our simplistic Cracker Jack example, we start to see an array of options that not only satisfy our initial ideas of what we want but also address the far more critical question of why we want it in the first place. When buying a car, you might tell a car dealer that you want a white car. Well, fine, but what if the model you like isn't available in white? Why did you want a white car? Is it because you appreciate the simple aesthetic? Are you concerned about keeping the car cooler in a warm-weather environment? Maybe you've bought into the myth that white cars don't get pulled over as frequently by law enforcement and want to limit the risk of a speeding ticket? Are you worried about resale value and recognize that white is by far the most popular car color in North America? If you really wanted the dealer to help you find the car that best meets your needs, you'd want to share why you came in with certain preferences.

It turns out that individuals and organizations are far better at focusing on *what* they want than *why* they want it. Focusing on interests, on the *why*, is simple but powerful, and while it seems pretty obvious, it is rarely used effectively by either individuals or organizations. Because of this, neither are as good at negotiation as they could be.

For example, a client negotiating a contract with an advertising agency may focus heavily on the agency's hourly rate, working diligently during a negotiation to drive down what the agency charges them for their services. The agency likely wants to charge more, and they can easily end up in a stalemate over the rate. Again, let's ask the question, "Why do they want a lower rate?" Even a slight change in our understanding can have a significant impact on the negotiation. Let's say the client wants to reduce overall costs of advertising. Might there be other ways to get there other than a purely distributive approach of reducing the hourly rate the agency charges? Could the agency be part of the solution for reducing costs on advertising without a reduction in their rate? Without a doubt! Maybe a shift from traditional to digital media could give the client better ad coverage at a lower cost overall? What if, in working together, the company realizes that a major cost was in licensing music for TV ads and together they decide to turn this item from a cost into a profit center? Maybe have bands compete to be featured in a commercial that creates national attention far beyond the TV ads themselves. Perhaps create a revenue sharing model so both company and ad agency benefit. Options exist just about everywhere, in every negotiation, and by jointly understanding the problem better it opens the door to both parties getting far more value than they anticipated. As a recent client said when they changed their negotiation approach from long, detailed presentations to focusing on the interests of the other party, "That changed the whole conversation! I learned exactly what they needed, and it made it a lot easier to actually find a deal that worked." The key is in making a fundamental shift away from aggressively pursuing what we want to exploring why we want it. Armed with that, the parties can then be far more open to the many ways a given problem can be solved.

Even the decision to embrace negotiation as a core competency faces this very challenge. Why do you or your organization want to become more adept at negotiation? It is critical to understand the value you are getting out of your current approach to negotiation, and to understand what more could be achieved, and why. This will help inform how you implement the Negotiation Capability Model and uniquely apply it to your organization and context. Negotiations and negotiation programs that solve the "why" problem—that are responsive to the underlying interests at play—prove quite durable and sustainable. If your leadership team decides to look for and find negotiation training, it's fair to assume that they want better negotiators in the organization, but for what reason? To increase sales? To better retain customers? To retain talented employees? To help in preparing for large organizational change? To reduce the amount of conflict across departments? To reduce product defects? Why, why, and more why. Even after you accept the premise that training is needed, it's critical to know what areas need to be assessed for negotiation capability and what an effective program would look like. Everything depends on your why. What measurable impact are you hoping an increased negotiation capability can achieve for your organization? Without knowing this *why*, the outcome achieved in the negotiation cannot be measured for success, cannot actually contribute to the goals of the organization.

Ultimately, building negotiation capability is about zeroing in on the core interests that need to be met. Interests, at the end of the day, are the primary motivator for our actions and decisions. This is equally true of the party we negotiate with. Once we focus our attention, our negotiation skills toward interests, it becomes clear that an integrative approach is a foundational and necessary part of the negotiation function in almost every situation.

While interests serve as a critical motivator, another significant influence in every negotiation is power.

The Role of Power

Power is a critical and mostly misunderstood dynamic in negotiation. Typically, as negotiators, we are taught to build our power before a negotiation starts by just about any means possible, then to use that power to leverage or "force" the other party into accepting what we want. Or to use our power to block the other party from forcing us to accept something we don't want. Either way, negotiating power is often seen as the most important aspect of a negotiation. There are a number of problems with the use of power as a way to succeed in negotiation.

First, power is primarily a tool used in a distributive approach to bargaining, as we discussed earlier. When a party believes the only way to get what they want is to find a way to take something from the other side (a win-lose outcome), power inevitably becomes the focus. Unfortunately, power begets power. If one party brings and applies power in a negotiation, the other party feels compelled to defend themselves, also with power. Soon, the negotiation is about making threats, withholding information (knowledge is power, after all!), inflicting pain, and generally trying to win by any means. Power struggles are well known to cost both parties a great deal. In labor negotiations, for example, it is rare for either party to "win" when a strike or lockout takes place—at best, each party simply tries to minimize their losses. Relying heavily on power typically leads to everyone seeing all negotiations as distributive, resulting in relatively poor agreements when agreements can be reached at all.

What is rarely understood is that power itself is highly unpredictable. In one moment, a party may believe they hold a powerful position and rely on it heavily, believing that power equates to winning. History has proven this to be quite false. While it is fairly easy to determine which party has more power on the surface, what cannot be predicted is how far any party will go to apply the power available to them. The willingness of each party to actually use the power they have is largely unknown, often by the parties themselves, until it's too late. The use of power often leads to rapid, and unexpected, escalation.

A few examples. In 1976 in Northern Ireland, an IRA member named Bobby Sands was sentenced to 14 years in prison for "criminal activity," i.e., terrorism. He was sent to Maze prison, a maximum-security jail, a place where the government had maximum power over prisoners to dictate every activity in their prison lives. Sands, seemingly without power while imprisoned in Maze, started a hunger strike, gaining national and international attention. This attention propelled him, during his hunger strike, to actually be elected to the British Parliament as an MP for Belfast, infuriating British authorities. Sands, and nine other hunger strikers, eventually died from starvation, galvanizing support for the IRA and swaying international opinion in their favor—all from a position of having virtually no "power." Sands took the little power he did have to an extreme that the British government, seemingly holding all the cards, could not overcome.

Historically, war has been the ultimate use of power. In the 1960s through the 1980s, two superpowers, the United States and the (then)

Soviet Union each fought a war that they lost and lost badly, when in each case they maintained massive superiority in weapons and resources. In Vietnam, the United States spent hundreds of billions of dollars and many lives, only to retreat in failure. The Soviet Union did exactly the same thing in Afghanistan, an expensive failure as well. Both faced opponents with less resources and fewer weapons. Their opponents, however, were more determined and willing to take many more risks, something the more powerful nations and their armies could simply not overcome. Power, in other words, has significant limitations as a strategy.

These examples are dramatic, intended to illustrate the endpoint—the logical (or illogical) outcome parties will face when power is the main driver of negotiations. In addition, it should be noted that power-based approaches are simply not sustainable. Unions cannot go on strike forever—strikes have closed companies; the wages and jobs have simply disappeared. Suppliers, even with monopolies, cannot force high prices indefinitely—companies will at some point find new suppliers or technologies to end their reliance on an unworkable relationship. Even where one side has significantly more power to enforce their will, it will not last long, as power struggles are simply not stable. Dictatorships, statistically, are the shortest-lived type of government.

More importantly, however, is understanding that power, and distributive bargaining in general, almost always results in suboptimal outcomes—for both parties. In an integrative bargaining process, the parties exchange a wide range of information so they both can gain value from the outcome. Often, as we said earlier, what is important to one party is less important to another and vice versa. Integrative bargaining, then, results in each party maximizing the value they receive by creating that value collaboratively.

Within distributive bargaining, however, the only information shared by a party will be the information designed to convince, force, or lead the other party toward giving them what they want, regardless of all else. Information on why the party wants something, or what the party's goals and objectives are, will be hidden out of fear that it can be used against the party. When one or both parties are trying to minimize what the other party knows, the outcome, inevitably, will be minimal gains for both parties.

In the 19th century, an Italian engineer and economist named Vilfredo Pareto described the Pareto frontier, or the Pareto curve of efficiency. When applied to negotiation in an economic exchange, he showed that there is a curve, or frontier, where maximum value has been achieved, as in Figure 2.2. Any settlement that lands on the Pareto curve means that regardless which party received the value, all value was allocated in the exchange.

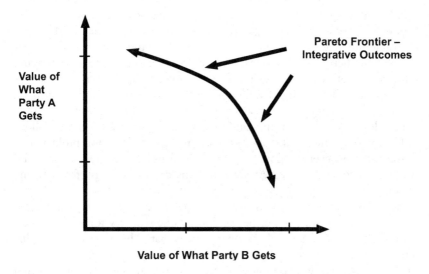

Figure 2.2 Pareto Curve of Efficiency in a Two-Party Negotiation

Unfortunately, most negotiated outcomes get nowhere near the Pareto frontier. In many negotiations, each party ends up receiving far less value than was available, as in Figure 2.3.

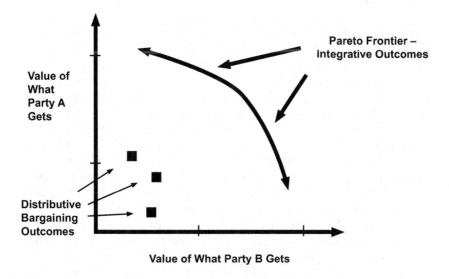

Figure 2.3 Suboptimal Outcomes in Distributive Bargaining

Why? What happens in a negotiation that causes this result? The answer is simple—when power is overused in a negotiation or when distributive bargaining becomes the default approach, both parties tend to suffer. Maximizing value in a negotiation requires parties to share more information rather than less. When parties are clear with each other on what they need and why, when both parties focus on meeting not only their own interests but those of the other parties as well, optimal solutions result. And by building negotiation processes where parties collaborate on both process and outcomes, long-term relationships and longer-term success also tend to follow.

It should be noted that power itself is neither bad nor problematic. Power exists in every negotiation and should not be ignored, but neither should it become the focus. At the end of the day, power exists for only one reason—as a tool that may help a party get its needs or interests met. Power is rarely an end in itself—it is merely a way to achieve or acquire what is needed. Seen this way, power becomes only one pathway for a party to get its interests met—and a high-risk pathway at that. There is an entirely different approach for a party to get its interests met, one that has a far higher success rate than relying on power. Integrative bargaining, without ignoring the power dynamic, can shift the focus directly toward interests, toward a problem-solving approach that can meet many more of both parties' interests than distributive bargaining can.[12]

One effective use of power is through the use of BATNA. BATNA is an acronym for "Best Alternative to No Agreement."[13] BATNA suggests this: we all think we negotiate for what we want, but this is only marginally true. In reality, BATNA tells us that we actually negotiate for the best alternative that is available to us, *whether we like it or not.*

In 2013 at a General Motors plant in Canada, the parties concluded a collective agreement that restricted the hiring of temporary workers. The union representing the workers felt they were in a strong bargaining (i.e., power) position and rejected any use of temporary workers, insisting that all new hires be brought in as full-time employees. GM, not wanting to risk a strike at that time, reluctantly agreed, as the assembly plant was running three shifts and demand was high. GM saw agreeing to this term as their best alternative when compared to a labor showdown at that time. In other words, reaching agreement was their BATNA at that moment. But, as we've said, power is fickle. GM was able to start increasing production shortly thereafter at another facility, creating a better alternative for them going forward. Not long after, through natural attrition, new employees were needed at the Canadian plant to keep the full three shifts running. GM approached the union and again requested the ability to hire temporary workers to give them more flexibility. The union again refused. GM now explained that they had a new alternative, which was simply to not hire anyone. While the new contract required any new hires to be brought in as full-time employees, it did not require GM to hire if they chose not to. GM explained that their new alternative was to shut down the third shift once they didn't have enough workers left to run it and lay off the remaining third shift workers. The union had exercised power to deny the temporary worker classification in bargaining, and now GM was exercising power in refusing to hire. The union refused to agree, staying with power (and likely believing GM was bluffing). Instead, GM shut down the third shift and laid off hundreds of full-time employees. A few months later, still not hiring, GM informed the union that they were having trouble staffing the second shift, and if still not allowed to hire temporary employees, they would close the second shift resulting in more layoffs and move that production to a different facility. This time, faced with a second round of layoffs because of this power-based negotiation (a very poor alternative for them), the union agreed to negotiate. Both parties came to the table, put their concerns forward, and agreed to the hiring of temporary workers with full union protection and a transition process to permanent employment within a defined period of time. Hundreds of temporary workers were hired, and the third shift was reinstated. GM achieved flexibility with the new temporary workers and the union achieved the reinstatement of the third shift along with benefits, seniority, and a path to permanent employment for the new temporary workers. GM responded to power with power of their own but kept the focus on interests, drawing both parties back down to integrative bargaining.

There are many forms of power in any negotiation, but all share one characteristic—it leads to distributive negotiations that will tend to get poor outcomes for both parties. In the General Motors example, it was only after both parties endured losses that a change to more integrative negotiations took place. A core competency for organizations is to train and focus the entire process of negotiation toward more integrative behaviors right from the beginning.

Underlying this shift toward an integrative approach, however, is another dimension to negotiation that is often overlooked. That dimension is the quality of the relationship between the parties.

Relationships

Two graduate students studying negotiation were assigned to play a ten-round Prisoners' Dilemma Game (much like the one described earlier, only a two-party version) where the outcome constituted 50% of their overall course grade and played out over ten weeks. Well-versed in navigating the cooperation/competition tension in maximizing their own success, they engaged in an exploratory "Tit For Tat" dance and were finding a fair amount of success in both playing the Y card. Their scores were growing. Before the final round of the game, they were allowed to discuss strategy to try to firm up any agreements. This was particularly noteworthy as this final round of negotiation carried with it a multiplier of ten times the value of any previous negotiation round. They had two other opportunities prior to this one to reach agreement together and had made deals that both had honored each time. Through their consistent behavior and transparent communication, they had earned each other's trust. Yet, this was the last round of the negotiation game, and one of the students recognized the opportunity this presented. By breaching an agreement, by agreeing to play Y but actually playing X when the time came, there were enormous gains to be had. It was the final round, the end of the assignment. The niceties no longer mattered so much. Sure enough, the strategy worked! This student played the X after agreeing to play Y and by surprising their partner this way earned the highest score in the negotiation game and, subsequently, the highest marks in the course. Yet, the win proved costly. Over the next 10+ years, the two found themselves crossing paths professionally, having to negotiate and problem-solve on behalf of their organizations. The losing student never forgave the winner, and they could never reestablish a good working relationship. Instead, any future negotiations (now with much higher stakes) became a referendum on the strained relationship from the past. Outcomes suffered. What was perceived as a simple transaction in a game at school actually led to a thorny relationship for many years.

A significant barrier in finding ongoing success in negotiation has to do with a mistaken belief that somehow, in each negotiation, we are forced to make a choice of either getting a better outcome and damaging the relationship with the other party, or accepting less and maintaining the relationship. So often this is seen as an either/or choice—negotiate hard and lose the relationship or be nice, agree to less, and keep the relationship. When negotiators see this as an either/or choice, regardless of which one is chosen, long-term value will suffer. In our earlier example, the two students actually had both—they were each getting strong results and the relationship between them was also strong. The student who breached the deal was set to receive an A in the class already without any deceptive negotiation tactics, yet decided to try for even more, knowing it would damage or end the relationship. He chose results over relationships, thinking that would lead to success. He won, but this narrow view of the value of relationships within the negotiation process led to significant issues for years to come. Failing to treat relationships as an important interest within the broader negotiation can have consequences, and costs, that may be difficult to reverse.

Often, this choice we face between relationships and outcomes is a false one—another pervasive myth that we must work to overcome. If we are solving negotiation challenges by focusing on interests, we can transparently pursue our own interests without the need for others to lose, without the need to overpower them, without the need to trick them. These are choices that negotiators often make because they fail to recognize that the true power, the true path to gaining value, is in the alignment of our interests. This is a power that can deliver outcomes while strengthening relationships at the same time.

Perhaps the most neglected but important relationship in a negotiation is the one an individual has with their own organization. When what is good for the individual negotiator is also good for the organization, when this relationship is strong and aligned, sustained success is possible. As we will explore further in the chapters ahead, these internal relationships are often the starting point, the foundation, for being able to consistently engage in complex problem-solving with our external negotiation partners.

True Self-Interest

Often, negotiations are derailed by that simple yet powerful drive we all have—self-interest. What's in it for me? Or, if you are craving another acronym—WIIFM? In negotiation, we expect that each of us is motivated to pursue outcomes favorable to our own interests. To the extent that our organization has aligned organizational interests with individual ones, then our WIIFM self-interest pursuit is not only good for us but also has us acting as a perfect agent for our organization.

Distributive bargaining is the mot obvious form of self-interest. Each party negotiates caring only about what they are getting, how it meets their own needs, without caring how well the other party does. As we saw in the Prisoner's Dilemma game, striving only to maximize our own interests, ironically, often leads to getting far less than we could have. In many cases, being exclusively self-interested isn't actually very, well, self-interested.

As paradoxical as it may seem, if what we care about is our own success, then we must spend considerable time and energy in understanding and caring about the needs of our negotiation partners across the table. True self-interest is achieved by paying attention to not just our own interests but the interests of the other party as well. The reason for this is simple: as a party to the negotiation, they, just like us, have great influence on what the outcome looks like. So even when we are primarily concerned with our own outcomes, concern for the other party's outcomes may prove to be the most effective path to get there. In other words, integrative negotiation brings with it a strong empathetic orientation—even if it is cognitive, not emotional, empathy.

This means that, arguably, the only path toward true self-interest in negotiation is by learning to become an empathetic negotiator. This is true for individuals and organizations alike. Both cognitive empathy—an ability to understand the needs and thoughts of the other party—and emotional empathy—an ability to understand the feelings of others involved in negotiations—are fundamental to our ability to navigate complex problem-solving as we go after our own interests. Put simply, to get your own interests met, you must be able to understand other people and their interests.

At the organizational and internal level, this empathetic path to achieving our own interests is equally important. The organization must understand the underlying interests of its negotiators and help make sure their interests are aligned. Individual negotiators need to ensure they understand what is important to the organization and work to ensure they are negotiating to that end. So often, this lack of cognitive and emotional alignment forces us to make assumptions that serve us poorly. We begin to create false dichotomies, such as assuming we must choose between the outcome of our negotiations or the relationships surrounding them.

This basic paradox is often the undoing of an organization's ability to negotiate well. They fail to recognize that they must pay attention to their own negotiator's interests and create the support structures that help them meet those interests. Instead, they often resort to rugged individualism, assuming that individuals will brave whatever barriers exist in the name of the organization. They fail to see what's actually important to their own negotiators, which in turn impacts the organization getting its needs met.

As we will learn in the chapters ahead, achieving true self-interest in negotiations will require a deep understanding and alignment with the interests of others.

Negotiation Styles

Often, we are asked a basic question—what is the most effective negotiation style? People are often looking for the best personality type or the best persona to assume during negotiations that will prove to be effective. They might have an image of a negotiator from popular culture that they feel exemplifies a smooth and effective talker and want some guidance on the path to becoming that individual.

Well, we have some good news and some bad news. First the bad news. There is no dominant negotiation style associated with negotiation success. Research has looked at business-like styles, friendly styles, analytical styles, and others, and none come out as more successful than any others.[14] This, interestingly, is the good news as well. The most effective style is the one that aligns with your organization's and your individual values. The style that allows you to be able to follow evidence-based negotiation principles, the style that supports an integrative approach in a way that works with, not against, the overall strategy and goals of your organization, is likely the best style. Choosing a style that aligns with individual and organizational values will be the one that is most likely produce success, as you define and measure it for your organization and yourself.

In other words, the key practices that drive negotiation success are far more strategic and process-oriented than they are stylistic. The choice to take an integrative approach is far more important than whether the tone is warm and friendly or cool and professional. Strategic choices may well intertwine with stylistic considerations and cultural overlays but, at the core, what leads to negotiation success rarely rests with the personal style choices of the individual negotiator.

This leads us to our final foundational element to consider—the role of complexity in the negotiation process.

Embracing Complexity

> For every complex problem there is an answer that is clear, simple—and wrong.[15]

Negotiation falls into this trap regularly. As people, our brains like certainty. When faced with complexity, many people are uncomfortable and reach for a simple, clear answer—that is wrong. That is actually a poor solution to the problem they face.

One of the attributes common to negotiators who fare poorly is that they tend to approach negotiations as a series of simple, discrete, and independent issues that can be solved quickly. They like the orderliness of a linear approach. Often, for example, they learn the simple tactic of trying to gain momentum in negotiations by solving all the easy issues first. While momentum might be useful at times, it is too simplistic to think that momentum alone can replace complex problem-solving. This approach of treating each issue within a negotiation as its own independent mini-negotiation can feel like progress (finding solutions on simpler issues) but might actually be building momentum toward a stalemate over the more important issues at play.

While taking the time to understand each other's needs might feel slower at first, it may actually be setting the stage for more genuine progress toward a durable agreement. In some cases, we must go slow to go fast. Unfortunately, keeping it simple and shallow isn't always great advice for negotiations and negotiation programs.

In addition to the underlying "why" questions that we need to ask, we need to understand our priorities and the priorities of others. Part of the complexity in negotiation that we must embrace is the idea that we don't care about every issue (or every negotiation) equally. Some issues are critically important, and others are more in the nice-to-have category. As part of our predisposition toward zero-sum thinking, we often assume that if an issue (or a negotiation) is of critical importance to us, it must be just as important to our negotiation counterparts as well. We gird ourselves for the fight instead of looking for solutions that actually provide value to both parties, something often called "logrolling"[16] or "dovetailing." In essence, logrolling is the exchange of taking less on one issue, usually less important in priority, for gain on another issue, usually one that is more important to us. This difference in preference or importance between the two issues results in an increase of the overall value for both parties. This dovetailing is a critical skill for integrative negotiation. It's also nearly impossible to implement at the individual level without understanding, deeply, the "why" for both parties, the priorities of both parties, and having the organizational alignment that we advocate in this book.

Think back to our Win As Much As You Can negotiation. Remember the personal losses that flowed from trying to maximize each individual round (or issue) without consideration of the other parties at the table? It is only when we embrace the relationship between cooperating and competing that we begin to move toward collaborating and the gains that come from a more complex, nuanced, problem-solving approach.

In a similar vein, your organization is at a major disadvantage if you treat each negotiation as an independent activity and predominantly the domain of the individual negotiator. It is only when we see negotiation as a more systemic, organizational activity that we begin to see our organization's negotiation competencies grow dramatically.

While often tempting to treat each negotiation as a standalone moment or to think of an individual negotiator as the primary or sole driver of negotiation success, it is only when we accept that all negotiations take place within an organizational framework that we start to create the type of negotiation success we aspire to have. The fundamental understanding that complexity itself brings many options and ideas into play is often the key to getting unstuck and unlocking the power of alignment.

Summary

The vast majority of negotiators believe that negotiation is their sole domain, and that the success or failure of their negotiations rests primarily with their own individual skill, strategy, and execution. This is a romanticized ideal of rugged individualism where an individual can bootstrap negotiation success on individual guts and guile. It is this fallacy that leads to fragmented behavior at the table that is unable to fully realize consistent negotiation successes.

There is a set of skills and abilities each individual must master to be an effective negotiator. In addition, organizations have a similar set of skills that must be mastered and operationalized. Individual skills and competencies matter, but they must be part of a larger strategic framework designed to build organizational capabilities. These must be aligned. It is in that alignment where the true power to realize negotiation success resides. The NCM is designed to do just that.

The following chapter will provide an overview of the NCM, outlining an approach for taking your organization from its current state to a well-aligned negotiation machine capable of repeatable success, adapting to the specific demands within your organization, and optimizing negotiations throughout your key partnerships and industry.

Notes

1 Walton, R. E., & McKersie, R. B. (1965). *A behavioral theory of labor negotiations.* McGraw-Hill.
2 Fisher, R., & Ury, W. (1981). *Getting to yes: Negotiating agreement without giving in.* Penguin Books.
3 It should be noted that throughout the book we use the words "negotiating" and "bargaining" interchangeably, notwithstanding that "bargaining" seems to have a more distributive feel to it. We see them as essentially the same process.

4 www.etymonline.com/word/compete

5 Ontario Civil Justice Review, Heather Cooper, Robert A. Blair, Ontario Court of Justice, 1996.

6 These numbers are higher now due to inflation, though the proportions are even worse today, as legal costs are estimated to have increased faster than the rate of inflation over the years.

7 www.pon.harvard.edu/shop/win-as-much-as-you-can/

8 https://plato.stanford.edu/entries/prisoner-dilemma/

9 Imhof, L. A., Fudenberg, D., & Nowak, M. A. (2007). Tit-for-tat or win-stay, lose-shift? *Journal of Theoretical Biology*, *247*(3), 574–580.

10 Please see the Wikipedia entry for Cracker Jack, if unfamiliar with this unique snack food—https://en.wikipedia.org/wiki/Cracker_Jack

11 https://the-big-bang-theory.com/rock-paper-scissors-lizard-spock/

12 For a detailed understanding of power, interests, and a third approach called "rights," see *The Conflict Resolution Toolbox*, Gary Furlong and Callan Furlong, Wiley and Sons, 2020, Chapter Four: The Stairway.

13 BATNA was coined by Roger Fisher and William Ury in "Getting To Yes," and originally stated it as" Best Alternative To a Negotiated Agreement." We have used the simpler version of this earlier acronym.

14 For an in-depth look at different personality and communication styles, see *The Conflict Resolution Toolbox*, Gary Furlong, 2020 Wiley and Sons, Chapter 11: The Social Style Model.

15 H. L. Mencken, various sources.

16 Tajima, M., & Fraser, N. M. (2001). Logrolling procedure for multi-issue negotiation. *Group Decision and Negotiation*, *10*(3), 217–235.

3 An Overview of the Negotiation Capability Model

In Chapter 1, we focused on assessing the quality of the negotiation processes currently in place. The Negotiation Assessment Tool (NAT), when applied, will clearly identify the activities and practices taking place in the organization and will help identify the level and quality of those practices. Establishing this baseline is critical in understanding your organization and seeing the areas and opportunities for improvement. If Ad Hockery is predominant, results will be unpredictable and chaotic. A few negotiations will go well (for reasons that are hard to know), many will be average at best, and the rest poor or even disastrous (also for reasons that are hard to know). Make no mistake, however, reasons will be found—after all, it's human instinct to find someone or something to blame.

Take, for example, a manager in charge of procuring computer chips for a wide range of appliances that the company manufactures. These chips, given their relatively low level of technology, are seen more as commodities in the marketplace. Prices tend to drop every year, and the company buys in quantity. As the procurement manager, they have little contact with senior management that decides product strategy, and their director has set reducing procurement costs as a deliverable for them, one that will help determine their bonus. During the most recent negotiation, they were ruthless with the supplier, aggressively reducing unit prices and demanding the deal get done quickly and efficiently. It was perceived as a win in the moment, and their director praised their success. Then the COVID-19 pandemic hit.

Suddenly, supply chains were thrown into shortage and the supplier began curtailing shipments, which impacted production levels at their company. When the procurement manager called the supplier, they were told their company would be supplied only after they had supplied their strategic partners in other industries, clients who had taken the time to integrate their supply chains for mutual benefit rather than buy primarily on price. The director, with perfect 20/20 hindsight, now questions the procurement manager's judgment in treating a critical supplier this way.

It's hard to fault the procurement manager since they clearly met their goals, and the pandemic took everyone by surprise. But looking more closely we can assess the actual reasons for the approach they took with this

DOI:10.4324/9781003243854-4

supplier. First, there was clear direction to reduce costs, with little discussion or consideration of benefit versus risk—only cost seemed to matter to the director. Second, this was reinforced by incentivizing them personally for cost reduction—their bonus was dependent on it. Finally, there was little overt discussion of product strategy with them. Even in their key role of procuring an essential component, very little strategic direction filtered down to them or influenced their approach to negotiations with this important supplier.

It's obvious that the easiest response in this situation is to simply blame the manager of procurement, perhaps transfer them to a different position and bring in a "better" negotiator. Problem solved, it would seem. Or would it really be solved?

Likely, it wouldn't be. If this organization were to conduct a NAT assessment, they would quickly find that the real problem is that their procurement negotiations have been conducted in an ad hoc manner. Replacing the manager would simply be an ad hoc solution, where the organization would be hoping the new person was "better" at the job—without having any framework for what "better" even means. It would simply be assuming that somehow the new negotiator would be better at muddling through the lack of structure or clarity that this organization clearly suffers from. The only thing predictable is the unpredictable nature of future negotiations if the organization remains in Ad Hockery.

This chapter is about what "better" actually means when negotiating. Or more precisely, developing a negotiation process that helps the organization know what "better" means in each and every negotiation and then implement a framework that delivers "better" each and every time. The Negotiation Capability Model (NCM) is that framework. The NCM makes negotiation both an organizational competency as well as an individual one.

The Negotiation Capability Model

The NCM starts by helping the organization develop a clear (even if simple) system, with repeatable negotiation behaviors and processes. Only when a repeatable approach to negotiations is in place can progress be made toward creating reliable and predictable results. Repeatable processes create the foundation for the next step—practices that are nimble, adaptable, and flexible, capable of delivering ever higher quality results reliably and predictably. Finally, in certain cases, results can be fully optimized through a partnered approach between the negotiating parties. All this while strengthening key relationships along the way.

But how do we get there? What are the markers, the directions we should be looking at to start establishing approaches to negotiation that work? What do we do differently on Monday morning? How do we break out of our win-lose mindsets and find ways to creatively problem-solve in our negotiations? Is there a guide that can at the very least point us in the right direction?

There is. The NCM is the starting point, a roadmap for identifying the direction, activities, and processes the organization can use to begin identifying and creating a negotiation framework that leads to repeatable, reliable outcomes. In fact, it designs negotiation success in the same way civil engineers design and build bridges and skyscrapers. Our process for designing bridges and buildings ensures these structures successfully deliver results; our process for designing negotiations should also deliver results each and every time. The NCM can help to engineer consistent success at the negotiating table.

Behavioral Engineering for the Negotiation Process

At the beginning of the book we introduced the idea of behavioral engineering, pioneered by Thomas Gilbert. Gilbert's book[1] focused on how and why people in some settings were exceptionally competent, and in other environments their performance was far from competent. His work demonstrated clearly that individual competencies and skills were simply not enough to produce consistent results, that the organization's own processes, capabilities and environment were a critical piece of the puzzle. He described and identified specific areas needed for both individual performance and organizational performance. The Behavioral Engineering Model (BEM) that he, and others, developed distinguishes between the skills and abilities that each individual brings to the table (their repertoire of behaviors) and the organizational context they operate within (the environmental supports, resources, and direction that the organization provides). His message was this: individual competence and success does not come from individual skills and abilities, it is the combination of those skills in conjunction with the organization's skills and abilities, the environment it creates, the resources it allocates, and the incentives it offers. Success comes only when the two are designed and aligned. And it is organizational competence that must come first, must take the lead, to produce consistent results.

Gilbert also researched exactly how organizations can create this environment for success; what organizational competencies must be met to deliver results over and over. Behavioral engineering was his answer. Since its inception, there have been more than a few different behavioral engineering approaches designed for different industries, different activities, and different types of organizations with great success, but none have focused directly and exclusively on the negotiation process. None have directly assessed how to engineer success before the negotiation begins, at the negotiation table, and after an agreement is reached. Until now.

That said, all BEMs have identified this core need to develop both individual skills and abilities alongside organizational resources and supports, separately and together. In the field of negotiation, this has been sorely lacking. As discussed in the Introduction, the field of negotiation has been directed by damaging myths, the most significant one being the myth that negotiation is fundamentally an individual activity. The myth of the individual negotiator has essentially sabotaged the field's ability to engineer success and has kept most organizations in a state of unproductive Ad Hockery. We aim to change that now.

The NCM—Organizational Competencies

Applying behavioral engineering to the negotiation process has identified three organizational competencies that set the stage for negotiation excellence. As identified earlier, implementing key organizational competencies is the critical first step to success. Three organizational competencies are required for effective negotiation, as identified in the NCM model. In this chapter, we'll give you an overview of these three organizational Key Performance Areas (KPAs), how they link to three individual KPAs, and outline where the highest leverage for designing success in negotiation is located.

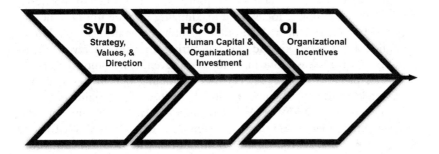

Figure 3.1 The NCM—Organizational Competencies

Strategy, Values, and Direction

The first organizational competency is Strategy, Values, and Direction (SVD). Negotiation, in the end, needs to be an enabler of the organization's strategy, an activity that furthers its goals and objectives. It may seem obvious, but negotiators need to be regularly engaged in discussions around the overall strategy of the organization, the direction on specific initiatives the organization has decided to undertake, and the overarching values the organization expects all staff, especially negotiators, to uphold.

Strategy takes many forms, depending on the context. Business strategy is critical—is the market strategy to be low-cost, high-volume, and high-market share? Is the strategy to focus on a niche market that is high-margin, low-volume, and low-market share? Where does service fit into the strategy? In our earlier procurement example, if the organization's strategy is to maintain significant market share for its appliances, then a guaranteed high-volume supply of computer chips with minimal chance of disruption would be a strategic goal. The negotiation strategy should have taken into account priority of supply, even if it cost a bit more per unit. Instead of the best outcome being the lowest price, the best outcome would be guaranteed supply at a fair price. Without a clear strategy guiding the negotiator, what appears to be a good outcome can instead be counterproductive.

Direction is an extension of strategy. While strategy tends to be overarching, direction is more tactical and narrower. If a product line is being phased out, for example, supplier terms should be negotiated that plan for this goal. If an organization is facing retention issues with staffing, its bargaining team will need to prioritize retention ideas in collective bargaining. Clear direction around specific issues or goals must be communicated, even overcommunicated, to bargaining leaders to ensure the organization's needs are met.

Values are also of critical importance to engage with and communicate to people leading negotiations. Many an organization has negotiated what it thought was a great deal, only to find that the deal itself violated the values that the organization espoused.

When Hertha BSC, a Berlin-based professional football club, was looking for a new sponsor, it focused on maximizing revenue from the deal. It negotiated an agreement with an online gambling operator, Bet-At-Home, to sponsor the players' kit and apparel, setting a record for revenue from sponsorship of this kind. But in its focus on revenue, it completely missed the values piece of the puzzle. Having a gambling operator as a sponsor was completely out of alignment with the values of its league affiliations and fan supporters. With Bet-At-Home now emblazoned on their apparel, jersey sales plummeted, and there were a number of matches where their kit wasn't permitted at all, reducing revenue from the new sponsor and requiring the club to produce and maintain a full set of uniforms without the new sponsor on the jerseys. The deal, which looked so good at the beginning, cost the club both fans and revenue, all because values weren't a part of the negotiation.

More recently, in 2018, it was revealed that Google was doing contract work for the US military, specifically assisting with data to support drone strikes. This from a company whose motto was simple: "Don't Be Evil."[2] Many employees of Google revolted—over 3,100 signed an open letter stating, "We believe Google should not be in the business of war." Three months later, after this embarrassing public spat with its own employees, Google did not renew its contract with the military. The leaders who negotiated that deal had not paid attention to the company's values beforehand and could have saved themselves a great deal of reputational harm as well as employee trust had they brought Google's values into the negotiation from the start.

The SVD practice area is the starting point, as it creates the overall organization-wide framework for establishing a negotiation process that serves the values, culture, and direction that the organization wishes to achieve. Organizational values are then reflected in each negotiation, strategic goals are established and pursued at the negotiation table, and negotiation as a skill set is valued as a critical organizational competency. The following goals and key concepts are focused around the SVD key performance area:

1. **Organizational values related to negotiation are identified and developed.** It must be crystal clear to everyone what the organization's values are, and what the high-level strategy for the organization is in relation to how it negotiates:

   - Does it primarily value "winning" a negotiation?
   - Does it value longer-term partnerships with suppliers and business partners? Does it value price? Reputation?
   - What does negotiation success mean in this organization? For each specific negotiation?
   - How important is the ongoing relationship with the parties in each negotiation?
   - What are the organization's ethical standards and practices?
   - How well are the organization's values represented in negotiation training programs?

   These may seem like obvious questions, yet every organization answers these questions by their choices and their behavior at the bargaining table. When these questions are answered clearly and explicitly, it starts to create a framework that shapes the direction of all future negotiations.

2. **Strategic negotiation processes, including planning and execution, are defined through specific procedures and practices that are implemented routinely in every negotiation.** This may include answering the following:

   - What planning and preparation steps *must* be executed for each and every negotiation?
   - What data must be gathered prior to and during the negotiation?
   - What must we know about the other party before going to the table?
   - How clearly have we identified our short- and long-term goals with each negotiation?

   Negotiations rarely succeed because of what happens at the bargaining table—they succeed proportionately to the amount and quality of preparation that takes place before the negotiation formally starts. Just as the negotiation itself cannot be left to the personal feelings of the negotiators on a given day, nor can the preparation process itself be left to the personal preferences of each negotiator. Preparation needs to be planned and defined, following a similar process each and every time. While the process can and should be scaled to match the complexity of each negotiation, the preparation process needs to be a repeatable and clear process followed for every negotiation.

Execution must also follow clear roles and responsibilities. The negotiator or negotiating team must have clear scope of authority to conduct bargaining, and this responsibility, along with appropriate authority, must be respected. At a large manufacturing firm, the negotiating team reached an agreement with a distributor that both parties felt met their interests well. Three days after reaching the agreement, the lead negotiator for the distributor called, asking why the manufacturer had unilaterally reduced their price, after signing an agreement, by another 1%? The manufacturer's negotiator made a few calls and found out their CEO had spoken to the CEO of the distributor and unilaterally offered them another 1%! Both negotiators felt they just had the rug pulled out from under them. When roles and authority aren't respected, it can undermine the relationship for years to come.

3. **Interest-based and integrative approaches to negotiation are prioritized.** While both integrative and distributive negotiations can be appropriate, the organization must understand that an integrative approach is much more successful at creating value for all parties and achieving long-term sustainable results. Distributive negotiations deliver short-term results that rarely build and sustain long-term strategy. For this reason, the negotiation-competent organization prioritizes and builds capacity for integrative, interest-based approaches as a primary strategy. This includes answering the following:

    - What value can be created in this negotiation for both parties?
    - How important is this relationship to the organization from a short-, medium-, and long-term perspective?
    - What interests, other than price, are we trying to get met?

    It is also true that not all negotiations will end up being integrative—it is not uncommon that one party will simply behave in a distributive manner. For this reason, having skills at distributive bargaining is also required, along with the ability to guide distributive approaches from one party back toward an integrative process.

4. **Clear measurements and key performance indicators (KPIs) for the negotiation process are in place and aligned with the organization's strategy and values**. This includes answering the following:

    - What are we measuring and why?
    - How do we know a negotiation was successful? What metrics will tell us that?
    - What measurements are meaningful for the broader negotiation process at our organization?
    - What goals were not achieved? Why?
    - How do we use these measurements to improve the next negotiation?

The importance of metrics, however simple, cannot be overemphasized. Without metrics that create a process of continuous evaluation and learning, the negotiation process will slowly slip back into reactive behaviors that keep the organization in Ad Hockery. In many ways, measurements and KPIs serve as quality control for the negotiation process, ensuring it has the same quality checks and balances as any product that is manufactured.

The importance of anchoring negotiations and decisions in clear SVD cannot be overstated. In 2021, after a decade of resisting significant public pressure from key stakeholders, Harvard University conceded and announced it would divest its then $41.9-billion-dollar endowment from direct investments in fossil fuels. For many years, the University had seemingly operated with only one value and direction—to maximize the return on their endowment. Even though Harvard espoused values of community, equity, and integrity, these simply were not seen to be applied to its investment behaviors. It took a decade and a great deal of reputational harm for Harvard to realize that their constituents expected these other values to be taken seriously as well. By not making sure their values, strategy, and direction were integrated into their investment negotiations, significant conflict and tension surrounded the university for more than a decade.[3]

Human Capital and Organizational Investment (HCOI)

Organizations invest significantly in many areas of their business, including real estate, equipment, IT infrastructure, recruitment and retention, training, and more. Yet how much is invested specifically in the human capital side of the negotiation function?

An effective negotiation team starts with hiring. How well has the company identified the skills or behavioral profile for the type of negotiators they are looking for? In other words, how generic versus how specific is it? The next is infrastructure. What kind of software or development tools have been provided to assist with negotiations? What kind of databases have been implemented to inform and support future negotiations? And staffing. Has staffing been properly assessed to give negotiators the resources they need to prepare effectively for every single negotiation?

One of the challenges for organizations is that the resources needed for effective negotiations are not simple to define. Unlike equipment needs or technical training, negotiation seems a "soft" activity, one that focuses, once again, on individual skills. While individual skills are an important part of the equation, the organizational side is critical and many times is missing. Time, for example. When does the negotiating team start preparations? A few days before negotiations start? A month? Experienced negotiators will often say that the day a contract is signed is the day negotiations start for the next one. Yet, how often is time allocated to collect important data from day one?

To illustrate, imagine a sports team trying to sell tickets to their events. This would seem to be a fairly simple transaction, not one that calls for a more interest-based or relational negotiation. But what if the team identified and gathered specific customer information into their customer relationship management (CRM) system that allowed them to understand the broader interests of their customers? Information such as: Why do they come to games? Are they avid fans or special event purchasers? Do they use this as a family experience? For business relationships? Furthermore, what do they value the most at the event—an easy parking experience, or do they bike to the stadium? How much do they typically spend on food and drink? There's no limit to the types of insights that can transform what appears to be a transactional ticket sale to a longer-term relationship-based negotiation. That switch in approach can also minimize attempts to make offers that simply won't resonate—like offering free beer to a group of teetotalers. This investment in improving data and information sets the stage for individual negotiators and leaders to have the information and tools needed for success.

To effectively meet more than short-term needs, investments in time and resources must be made, from hiring decisions to human resource policies and procedures, to preparation processes and IT support, to staffing needs. If negotiation is seen solely as an ancillary or secondary activity, the lack of investment will greatly impact the ability to be successful. As with most areas of every organization, properly deployed resources improve results. Negotiations must be seen this way as well.

So what, specifically, should an organization be focused on and investing in? The following areas and key concepts will guide the organization toward strengthening and supporting its human capital in the negotiation function.

1. **Hiring criteria for negotiation staff is developed based on organizational values.**

    Hiring right is the starting point for long-term success in negotiations. Most hiring processes, however, take the wrong approach when hiring negotiators. The emphasis typically falls on finding experienced negotiators—which seems obvious. Unfortunately, this means the focus becomes past negotiating experience and success. Yet hiring a negotiator who comes from an environment of "negotiating as winning," or an environment of "negotiator as lone wolf," or an environment where core values were simply not paid attention to will import the worst habits possible. This approach will perpetuate a "win some, lose some" mentality that leads us back to Ad Hockery. Effective hiring should focus on the following questions:

    • What does the candidate see as core values for the negotiation function?
    • What were the strategic goals of the negotiations they led in the past? Can they articulate these clearly?

- What fundamental approach, integrative or distributive, do they take in their work? Can they articulate integrative approaches they have used?
- How much time and importance do they place on preparation and data gathering?
- How self-reflective are they, and how do they improve their approach and skills on an ongoing basis?
- How structured is their preparation process?

2. **Human resource processes are designed to support the negotiation function.**

   Negotiation is a function somewhat different from most other operational functions in an organization. Frequently, negotiators feel they are alone on an island within the organization and often not understood by the many departments they negotiate on behalf of. This sense of isolation often reinforces an individualistic approach to the job and needs to be addressed through robust human resource processes that support the specific needs of negotiators. Effective human resource support should focus on the following questions:

   - How is performance evaluated for negotiators? How much focus is on results versus good process?
   - What is the promotion and career path for people with negotiation responsibilities? How is that skill set supported and nurtured?
   - How is high performance as a negotiator recognized? Acknowledged?
   - How much access to senior management do negotiators have?

3. **Investment is budgeted for identified training, tools, and materials needed to support the negotiation function.**

   In many ways, we spend money on what we see as important. It's no different in how we treat the negotiation function in the organization. Investment must be made to support the full range of activities we expect to be implemented if we want to see long-term success. A lead negotiator on a $50-million-dollar account described to us how he was also responsible for booking dates with the other party's executive assistant for the negotiations, for arranging rooms at a nearby hotel, and photocopying and binding presentation materials for the sessions—a distracting and poor use of a negotiator's time. To achieve high-level outcomes regularly, the organization needs to focus on answering these basic questions:

   - Does the assigned workload and timelines allow the time necessary for preparation and planning?
   - What kind of software, databases, and measurement tools are available for negotiators to use?
   - What kind of administrative support is offered or in place?
   - How well-developed are the training resources for negotiators? Is training done in-house or outsourced? How well are the

organization's values embedded in negotiator training? Do we simply send negotiators to event-style generic training as a perk?

- What kind of mentoring process is available to build skills on a continuous basis?

4. **Roles and responsibilities are clearly defined at all levels of the negotiation function.**

It should be clear that responsibility for sitting at the table and reaching an agreement falls on the lead negotiator on that file. That said, there also needs to be clarity on a number of other roles and responsibilities within the negotiation process from start to finish. For example:

- Who is responsible for researching past agreements, history with a supplier or partner, and gathering research on market conditions?
- Who is responsible for ensuring clarity on the primary goals of each negotiation?
- Who defines and identifies the most important interests to be achieved with each negotiation? What is that process, and who leads it?
- Who has authority to make decisions at the table, and what is the scope of that authority?
- Who is accountable for conducting a full debrief of each negotiation?
- Who communicates the outcome, deal terms, changes, accountabilities, and reasons for these to all relevant parties in the organization?

5. **Measurements and KPIs are collected organization-wide and audited regularly.**

Once metrics have been established and negotiators regularly use KPIs in their practice, a wealth of data and information is available. This data must be reviewed and mined for organizational learning, feedback, and continuous improvement. Questions include:

- What activities are necessary and contributing to negotiation success? How are these measured?
- What activities are not value-add and should be changed or dropped? How do we know?
- How effectively are the organization's values and strategy being achieved? What tells us this?
- How accessible is the negotiation data for staff who would benefit from it?

Human capital is the lifeblood of the negotiation function. Since negotiations are conducted by a small number of people in the organization, there is a great deal of reliance placed on them. Supporting the negotiation function in a planned and structured way is the only way to ensure ongoing success and improvement.

Organizational Incentives (OI)

A narrower organizational capability is the question of incentives. Just about every policy, every communication, and every activity that is regularly repeated in an organization creates incentives, and incentives will largely determine behavior.

Incentives can be both monetary and nonmonetary in nature. Monetary incentives are powerful in directing behavior, often taking precedent. Stories are legion, however, about the unintended consequences of monetary incentives. For example, an organization sees that one product's sales have slowed down, creating a glut of that product. They increase the commission on selling that product while also clearly telling the sales team to focus on selling their flagship product to build market share. Of course, the higher commissioned product begins to sell like hotcakes, while the flagship product languishes. Repeated messages, even threats, are issued to encourage sales of the flagship product, to no avail. By magnifying one incentive, behavior will follow regardless of other directives. As the saying goes, actions speak louder than words.

Incentives can also be nonmonetary. What is the career progression for effective negotiators? If being promoted to a senior management role means that their role as a negotiator is finished, this may be a clear disincentive to seek promotion or even stay with the firm. Where do negotiators report in the organizational structure? Reporting lines are often seen as a proxy for importance. If negotiators rarely get face time with senior leaders, it will be clear the organization places a low value on the function. If negotiators are connected into the higher levels of the organization, this higher status will be seen as an important benefit.

Measurements are subtle yet powerful incentives. It has become a truism that what gets measured gets done. The fact that a particular behavior or outcome is being measured brings attention and focus to that outcome and often creates unconscious incentives.

Incentives are simply motivators, and before incentives are even considered, the organization should understand the types of motivators that have the most traction with negotiation staff. Overall, an organization needs to understand the incentives that will motivate the people, the negotiators, in their organization. What are the goals, dreams, and interests of these people? What makes them tick, gets them out of bed in the morning? What are they trying to achieve, what do they see as an important contribution?

An obvious starting place is the type of organization itself. In a nonprofit organization serving vulnerable people, money and bonuses would likely be a disincentive rather than an incentive. In an investment banking environment, however, money would likely be high on the list of incentives. But care must be taken in both cases to not make assumptions. Understanding the motivators in each organization is the starting point, followed by aligning those motivators with policies and processes that move the organization in the direction it wishes to go. In fact, even an earnest attempt to create incentives with the "wrong" motivational carrots can create the opposite behavior. So part of an ongoing assessment is to understand what incentives will drive the desired behavior within the organization and to ensure that they are aligned to the type of outcomes that serve the organization's interests. Fundamentally, it is a critical organizational capability that incentives are created and designed to further the SVD of the organization.

In a large hospital operating room that performed elective surgery, there was a shortage of nurses. This resulted in the current nurses working significant overtime, greatly increasing their income but also creating burnout in many staff. The hospital, focusing on budget overruns, decided to create a night shift, which they were confident would reduce overtime since surgeries could be done at straight time on the night shift. They met with the nurses' union to reinforce that the loss of overtime for the nurses was not a contractual right, that the hospital was entitled to change the schedule, and to tell the union this change was better for the nurses as well. They failed, unfortunately, to find out the real motivators for their nursing staff, assuming that by reducing overtime and potential burnout, nurses would be happy. It turned out, however, that these operating room nurses were largely motivated by avoiding the shift work common to other departments—almost all elective surgery was done on a consistent day shift, making childcare and other family issues easier to manage. The fact that overtime would be reduced was a good thing, but having to work nights was a deal breaker. Recent hires started leaving, and new hires were even harder to come by. The hospital was forced to rethink the strategy quickly.

The OI practice area recognizes that people are fundamentally motivated by what they see as their interests. These interests include their personal interests—what benefits them individually—and their broader interests—what benefits the organization, their colleagues, society, and so on. Incentives can focus on any kind of interest, but the personal interests of the staff are ignored at the organization's peril.

Take, for example, a typical salesperson whose compensation is a combination of base salary and commission. This role is typically incentivized toward increasing sales by a commission structure that can be designed in one of two broad ways—the base salary can be minimal and is combined with a high percentage commission on each sale, or it can provide a higher base salary with a smaller commission on each sale. It may well result in very similar costs to the organization in terms of dollars per sales volume. However, in the first instance, each salesperson may be motivated to close every sale without taking the time to build a longer-term relationship with the client simply because they want to move quickly on to the next sale. In the second instance, the salesperson may be motivated to spend more time with the client, ensuring a second sale at a later date, since they don't feel the same level of monetary pressure to close every deal quickly.

Career path is a powerful nonmonetary incentive for many people. Often, employees feel that the only way to advance their career is to look for a job at a higher level with a different organization, something that erodes the retention of talented staff. By transparently creating a career path for negotiation staff, an incentive to stay and build a career can be an effective approach that maximizes retention and minimizes turnover.

So what, specifically, should an organization be focused on around the design of incentives? The following areas and themes will guide the organization toward alignment with direct and indirect incentives.

1. **Incentives are designed in alignment with the organization's SVD.**
   Make no mistake, incentives exist in every organization. The only question is this—were they implemented consciously, or have they simply developed as a by-product of other decisions? The negotiation function should be answering these questions:

   - What direct monetary incentives, if any, should the organization consider? How would these incentives align with the values of the organization? What behavior would they likely cause or privilege?
   - What indirect incentives currently exist? Are these incentives in alignment with the strategy and direction of the organization?
   - What actually serves as an incentive for staff in the negotiation function? How do we know?

2. **Incentives are tested and measured regularly to ensure continuing alignment with SVD.**
   Given the frequency of unintended consequences, incentive programs can be at high risk of creating outcomes that offset any benefits the organization thinks it is aiming for. Essentially:

   - How are we measuring the consequences of the incentives we have implemented? Are they doing what was expected?
   - What feedback are we gathering from negotiation staff about their interests, goals, and motivators? About how they think the current incentives are working for them?

3. **Career progression is designed and communicated to ensure staff retention is maximized.**
   When the future path isn't clear, the grass will always look greener elsewhere. Negotiation staff should see a clear progression for their career to minimize turnover of valued employees.

   - What are the long-term pathways for negotiators in the organization?
   - Is moving into management the only way to advance? Would this mean less (or even zero) time spent negotiating?
   - What other options may be available, and what options might staff actually be looking for?

Ensuring incentives are well designed and monitored is a key competency for every organization.

Summary—Three Organizational Capabilities

To properly engineer a successful negotiation process, organizational capabilities must take the lead but must be closely followed by addressing individual competencies. Next, we link these organizational capabilities to the individual competencies that must also be present.

The NCM—Individual Competencies

While organizational capabilities are often the missing pieces of the negotiation puzzle, the individual side is also critical to success. Each organizational capability has a matching individual capability that must be in alignment to achieve powerful outcomes regularly. Some of these individual capabilities are more familiar, as they include the skills and tools often taught in mainstream negotiation training. They go well beyond this, however, requiring a strong sense of fit within an organization, along with individual investment in success and a clear alignment of individual interests with Organizational Incentives.

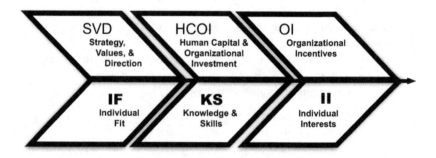

Figure 3.2 The NCM—Individual Competencies

Individual Fit (IF)

Fit is a critical concept in the NCM and one of the harder capabilities to address. That said, on one level, fit is rather simple—is each individual who leads negotiations committed to the philosophy and approach the organization takes to the negotiation process? Do they fit within the culture, do they support and practice negotiation in the way the organization has established? For example, if the organization promotes an integrative approach to negotiation and problem-solving, does the negotiator practice this approach at the table, or do they simply default to a distributive approach when push comes to shove? Individual Fit is directly linked to the SVD performance area.

The individual negotiator myth tells us that each negotiator must be free to negotiate in any way that works for them, as long as they deliver "results." As discussed, this is the path back to Ad Hockery. Being able to negotiate within the framework established by the organization is a required individual competence, accepting that there is plenty of freedom to succeed at the table within that framework. Fit is the essence of alignment.

Fit will also be strong when individuals are invested in the organization's negotiation processes. This is often demonstrated by behaviors that enhance both individual and organizational capabilities, such as:

- Self-reflection and a commitment to continuous learning
- Ongoing input into strategy and direction
- A commitment to both following and critiquing the negotiation framework of the organization
- Developing and following the roles and responsibilities of all parties in the negotiation process

The IF performance area is the high-level commitment framework for individuals in the negotiation function. Once SVD has established clear strategy and direction, IF ensures that individuals accept, understand, and practice their negotiations based on these directions. In addition, it ensures that at a deeper level, individuals understand, support, and demonstrate the organization's values and culture in all activities on behalf of the organization.

SVD establishes clear expectations by establishing specific practices, procedures, roles, and responsibilities that at their core are simply not optional. The IF performance area ensures that all negotiators understand and commit to following and furthering these practices.

In a large government office, the director and the union president simply could not work together. The director took a heavy-handed approach to dealing with the union president, who took an equally heavy-handed approach in resisting anything the director tried to change or implement. A long, painful stalemate went on for over a year. A consultant was brought in to try and change the win-lose mentality the parties had each taken to heart. Through a series of meetings and interventions with the leadership team and the executive of the union, new processes were put in place, a clear set of common interests was identified by the parties, and the parties met regularly to address issues quickly when they arose. Within four months, grievances dropped dramatically, and both parties felt the working relationship was significantly improved. Quite suddenly, however, the union president resigned his position. When the consultant met with him and asked what was wrong, he said not only was nothing wrong, he was very pleased with the new direction both parties were taking. When asked why, then, he was stepping down, he asked if the consultant had seen "The Godfather" movies, directed by Francis Ford Coppola. The consultant had. "Well," he said, "you might remember the scene where one of the Godfather's top lieutenants also stepped aside, telling the Godfather that he made 'a better wartime lieutenant than he did a peacetime lieutenant'. I'm the same. It's going in a much better direction, but collaborating is not what I'm good at—I'll leave it to others." He realized that his approach just wasn't a fit for the parties' continued collaboration.

So, what are the individual negotiator's goals and accountabilities needed to demonstrate fit across the negotiation function? The following areas and themes identify what is needed from individual negotiators.

1. **Organizational values are clear and understood.** Individuals must understand and demonstrate their willingness to follow the SVD the organization has established. For example:

   - How do organizational values affect and influence individual behavior before, during, and after each negotiation?
   - How do individuals define success in each negotiation?
   - Do individual negotiators accept and embody organizational values in their negotiations?

2. **Strategic negotiation practices and processes, including planning and preparation, are routinely implemented by individual negotiators in every negotiation.**
   This includes individuals demonstrating the following in practice:

   - Specific planning and preparation steps are executed for each and every negotiation
   - Relevant data is gathered prior to and during the negotiation
   - Relevant background knowledge is gathered about the other party before going to the table
   - Short- and long-term goals have been identified, validated, and accepted for each negotiation

3. **Interest-based and integrative approaches to negotiation are understood and applied.**
   While negotiators are able to engage in both integrative and distributive negotiations, individuals understand that an integrative approach creates greater value for all parties and typically results in longer-term, sustainable results. Individual negotiators are aligned and comfortable with integrative and collaborative approaches at the table. This includes being able to routinely answer the following:

   - What additional value can be created in this negotiation for both parties?
   - How important is this relationship to the organization in the short-, medium-, and long-term?

- What interests, other than price, can be met in this negotiation?
- How can I build and strengthen this relationship by the end of the negotiation?
- Even where a distributive approach is a better strategy, how do I maintain a positive relationship with the other party in spite of this?

4. **Measurements and KPIs for the negotiation process are welcomed and integrated into individual practice.**
   Measurements and KPIs are often seen as intrusive and a waste of time, or worse, as a means for the organization to criticize or find fault with an individual's performance. Individuals who are aligned with the strategy and values of effective negotiation see measurement not as an imposition but as the foundation of long-term success. Individuals are committed to answering:

- How will I know a negotiation was successful? What measurements will tell me that?
- What performance indicators should I be focused on for each negotiation?
- How can I use these metrics to improve my next negotiation?

Knowledge and Skills (KS)

As stated many times, individual negotiation skills are a requirement, a sort of price of admission. To support this, individuals must have access to effective, comprehensive training that teaches and refreshes the skills and competencies needed at the negotiation table. At minimum, these competencies must include a foundation in both integrative and distributive bargaining principles, with an emphasis on the skills needed to engage and lead integrative negotiations. Knowledge and Skills is directly linked to the HCOI organizational capability.

Training is only the starting point. In addition, negotiators need access to mentors and time to engage with and learn from peers as well. Negotiation skills are dynamic and must be used, practiced, and reflected upon to stay current and effective.

Take, for example, a major fast-food chain and their real estate division. At the core of their corporate strategy was the massive real estate portfolio they owned, bringing with it the many complex negotiations needed to grow their footprint and build stores for both their corporate-owned sites and their franchise-owned sites. Recognizing the need for advanced negotiation skills and capabilities, they invested heavily in a customized negotiation training program created and delivered by top negotiation trainers. The training was great! It was well received by the attendees and resonated. The trainers got rave reviews, and everyone was excited to put their new knowledge and skills into practice. Yet, the six months right after the training proved to be frustrating, with the real estate negotiation team concluding that "this stuff just doesn't work in the real world!" Every time they tried to use their new skills they would run into a range of significant internal barriers—lack of data, lack of a clear and specific mandate, the corporate strategy and actual incentives taking them in two different directions, no time or resources for proper preparation, and no support for focusing on metrics or measurements. They had failed to do the organizational work around SVD, HCOI, and OI; their individual knowledge and skills couldn't overcome this lack of organizational alignment.

SVD establishes the high-level values and direction for the negotiation function, and IF ensures that all individuals are a fit on a philosophical and values basis. HCOI makes sure the organization puts its money where its values are by hiring, funding, and investing in the necessary people and infrastructure that will ensure success. KS, in many ways, is where the negotiating rubber meets the road—but first, there needs to be a road! KS completes this picture by ensuring that these resources are applied effectively, that the skills and tools are indeed put into practice. These practices are then measured and reflected on regularly to ensure a culture of ongoing improvement.

So what are the individual negotiator's skills, abilities, and commitments needed to activate the resources HCOI has put in place? The following areas and themes identify what is needed from individual negotiators.

1. **Negotiation roles and responsibilities are understood and accepted.** Individuals must understand both theirs and other's roles and responsibilities in the negotiation process. For example:

    • Who is accountable for setting goals and markers for success in each negotiation?
    • Who conducts research and data gathering?
    • Who ensures organizational values are embedded in the negotiation strategy?

2. **Individuals are trained, mentored, and assessed against a base of measurable skills and abilities.**
    There are myriad skills that are taught in many generic negotiation courses, and many of these skills are important and necessary. They rarely, however, are organized into a clear body of Knowledge and Skills that each negotiator is expected to be able to perform. Individuals must clearly understand:

    • What skills must I be practiced at and able to apply when needed?
    • What knowledge is required in my work as a negotiator?
    • How do I regularly assess and improve my own skills?

3. **Individuals have the ability to follow and apply the practices and procedures established for the negotiation process.**
    It is one thing to establish a clear set of procedures for preparation, data gathering, and leading the negotiation process at the table. It is another thing to ensure that individuals have the knowledge, skills, and commitment to apply them effectively:

    -   What training, support, or mentoring is needed to ensure individual negotiators understand and can apply the expected negotiation processes in the organization?

4. **Individuals give regular feedback on improving the negotiation approach and process in the organization.**
    In addition to applying the process, negotiation staff must also participate in improving the way negotiation is practiced by regularly giving feedback aimed at continuous learning at the organizational level.

    -   What would improve the processes, policies, or procedures in the organization?
    -   Where is additional investment needed to strengthen the negotiation function?

5. **Individuals are trained and skilled at using measurements and KPIs in all aspects of the negotiation process.**
    Once the use of data and KPIs is seen as integral to the negotiation process, each individual negotiator must have the ability to implement the measurements, gather information and then apply the data before, during, and after each negotiation.

    -   How is each KPI implemented? When and how is the information gathered?
    -   How can each KPI be used before and during each negotiation?
    -   How can these metrics be used to improve the next negotiation?

Individual Interests (II)

Finally, each individual's interests must be in full alignment with Organizational Incentives for both parties to be successful. Echoing the need for Organizational Incentives to create the desired behaviors, individual needs and goals must be aligned with the organization's, both on the monetary and the nonmonetary sides. Individual Interests is directly linked to the OI performance area.

Imagine the scenario that plays out over and over in intercollegiate athletics. Coaches are hired by the university and told to win on the playing field, maintain the player's outstanding academic performance in the classroom, ensure the athletes are model citizens within the community and prepared to launch meaningful careers upon graduation (and yes, make sure they graduate!), and have an experience that supports physical and mental well-being. University presidents, athletic directors, and other key stakeholders are consistently direct and clear in setting these priorities—until you review the coaching contracts. By and large, the vast majority of financial incentives and bonuses are about winning on the field. While the contract may have language in a number of these areas, the contracts' actual incentives and priorities lie in one area—winning. And for icing on the incentive cake, coaches are recruited by larger schools and paid even more money based almost exclusively on how often they win.

"Mixed motive" problems are common within organizations, on two levels. On the nonmonetary side, negotiators, as all other employees, look ahead to where their career path may be going. Organizations that fail to pay attention to understanding the longer-range goals of their negotiation staff risk either losing them or having them focus their behaviors on their personal objectives instead of, or even in opposition to, the organization's goals. Effective career planning includes training and educational objectives, type of assignments, and performance feedback. Regular reviews that solicit individual feedback will result in rebalancing nonmonetary incentives and goals, which ensures alignment and performance.

On the monetary side, great care must be taken to ensure alignment around performance bonuses, pay scales, and any other monetary incentives that may exist. Compensation is the most obvious. What is the compensation structure for negotiators? Is there a direct link between individual compensation and finalizing contracts? What do individuals see as important in the negotiation process? If the incentive is to "close deals," whether these deals are in sales, procurement, hiring, or other areas, deals will be closed—but whether that is actually what individual negotiators think is wise may be an issue. In some cases, walking away from a deal is actually the right decision—but simply won't happen if the lead negotiators feel they are directed to get an agreement no matter what. Even without a direct link from closing deals to personal income, if people who negotiate deals quickly are promoted, this incentive will drive behavior. Individuals, in other words, must be engaged regularly for feedback on their interests, on what they see as important, and how they see those interests fitting within the organization.

Historically, organizations set up incentive programs, create compensation plans, and promote and hire as they see fit, or as the consultants they hire see fit. Often, these decisions are made without a great deal of consultation or information directly from the people who are most affected by these decisions. It is simply expected that individuals will accept and fit into whatever the organization creates and establishes. Often, these programs fail to evaluate whether they are even achieving their desired outcomes.

When individuals begin to see that their interests are taken into account, that they are expected to share their personal goals and discuss alignment with the organization's incentive processes, these areas can actually be strengthened effectively.

To align Organizational Incentives with Individual Interests, the following key concepts need to be addressed.

1. **Individual Interests, goals, and motives are communicated and addressed regularly.**
   Individuals must feel a sense of safety that is strong enough to have them share their important interests and goals with the organization on a regular basis. Answers to these questions are critical to share:

   • What are the most important interests I have in my role as a negotiator?
   • What are my career goals? What can the organization do to help me with that?

2. **Individuals respond positively to Organizational Incentives.**
   Regardless of the intent behind any organizational incentive plan or process, individuals must see these as actually creating a positive incentive. Answers to these questions are critical to gather:

   • What do I feel motivated to do, based on monetary incentives?
   • What do I see the organization's policies and processes directing me toward and why?

3. **Individuals have a clear and safe pathway for identifying misaligned incentives.**
   When disincentives occur, individuals must flag these issues quickly to allow a chance for change. Answers to this question are critical:

   • What is the process for raising and addressing issues when disincentives or demotivating situations arise?

Implementing the NCM—Organizational Capabilities First

In the next chapter, we'll be going into greater depth on each of the six KPAs that are represented in the NCM. Before the deep dive, however, it may be helpful to understand the impact each capability can have and understand the most effective sequence for implementing the NCM in an organization. The six capabilities are not all created equally when it comes to impact. In fact, the sequence for making changes based on the NCM is important. In other words, some of the capabilities should be implemented before others if we are to gain that all-important advantage—leverage.

The organizational competencies in the NCM are focused into these three main areas: strategy, investment, and incentives. Strategy creates the foundation for clear direction, focus, and decision-making. Investment provides the needed time, tools, infrastructure, information, hiring, and training. Incentives ensure that organizational rewards and compensation channel negotiators in the direction of the desired outcomes. All three of these provide leverage, in varying degrees, to changing and improving results.

The individual competencies are focused into three complementary and linked areas: fit, skills, and individual interests. Fit ensures that each individual is aligned with the philosophy and culture of the organization and is committed to implementing and following the structures and processes established by the organization. The skills area ensures that training in the knowledge and skills needed for both negotiation and content are aligned with the organization's strategy. Individual Interests are explored to ensure alignment with the Organizational Incentives that have been put in place.

As we have seen, each organizational practice area is directly linked to a specific individual competency area—one supports the other. This gives us three paired practice areas as follows:

- Strategy, Values, and Direction at the organizational level are paired with Individual Fit at the individual competence level;
- Human Capital and Organizational Investment at the organizational level is paired with Knowledge and Skills at the individual competence level;
- Organizational Incentives at the organizational level are paired with Individual Interests at the individual competence level.

These three paired capabilities, organizational linked to individual, form the most effective stepping stones to put in place when implementing change.

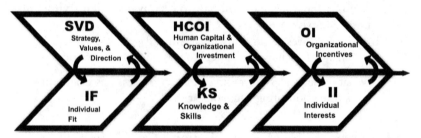

Figure 3.3 Organizational and Individual NCM Alignment

There is also an important sequence between these three stepping stones that will facilitate change most effectively. This sequence starts at the strategy level with Strategy, Values, and Direction and Individual Fit, followed by a focus on people through Human Capital and Organizational Investment and Knowledge and Skills, and finishes with the creation and alignment of Organizational Incentives and Individual Interests.

Why does this sequence—SVD/IF to HCOI/KS to OI/II—matter? Quite simply, leverage and return on investment. The highest leverage at the lowest cost is in the SVD area. Setting clear strategy, defining what a "good" outcome is, and prioritizing the goals that are aligned with the values and direction of the organization will have an immediate impact on the thinking, approach, and execution of every negotiation the organization engages in. Then, to maximize impact, SVD is aligned with the individual

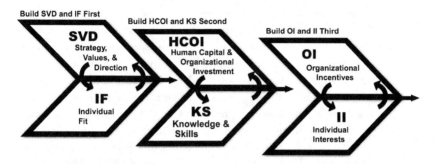

Figure 3.4 Sequencing the KPAs

competence of Individual Fit (IF). Step one, then, for implementation is to establish SVD, followed by ensuring Individual Fit is fully aligned. Note that focusing first on clear SVD is not only the highest leverage to change the negotiation process, but it is also relatively quick to do, as most organizations have a well-defined business strategy and/or philosophy in place already.

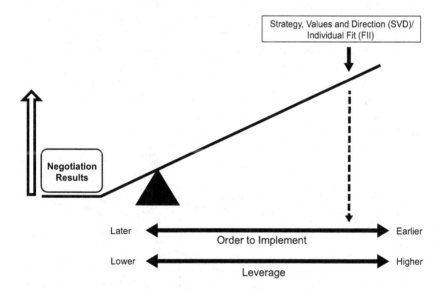

Figure 3.5 Leveraging SVD and IF for Results[4]

Imagine a professional sports team that relies heavily on corporate sponsorship as a revenue stream. For years, the basic model looked like this: companies would buy signage and luxury boxes at a premium cost, delivering significant revenue to the team. Clients seemed happy to greenlight the sponsorship agreements and few questions were asked about the true value of these sponsorships. In recent years, however, sponsorship dollars have begun to dry up. Companies have started questioning their own decision-making for such a luxury spend on a sports property. The sports teams are now having to take a hard look at this value proposition and must look to negotiate this value in a completely different way. What if the sports property begins to shift from sponsorship (a one-sided spend by a company for specific benefits from the team) to a partnership model (identifying specific business goals for the client that align with the goals of the sports team, with both parties having accountability for delivering results)? Can the sports team become a de facto business consultant, delivering clear returns on investment to their partners while also generating revenue for the team? It can and it has. But the path begins with this key negotiation strategy—an SVD starting point, along with individual negotiators who understand and support this approach that sets the stage for a fundamentally different approach to this negotiation.

Human Capital and Organizational Investment, aligned with Knowledge and Skills, are next. Using the analogy of putting the organization's money where its mouth is, strategy is the mouth, and investment is the money. Impact and leverage with HCOI and KS are also fairly high, though the cost and time to implement are also higher. Take hiring, for example. Some of the most significant human resource costs are in hiring, onboarding and orienting new staff, followed by ongoing training and mentoring toward delivering high performance and high value for the organization. Few costs are as great as investing significant time and money in the hiring process only to find in the first few years that the individual was a bad hire. After HCOI is clear and established, the companion competency of KS needs to come next. The knowledge, skills, and abilities demonstrated by individual negotiators must align directly with the HCOI. This will take longer to implement but will add significant leverage in helping the organization deliver results.

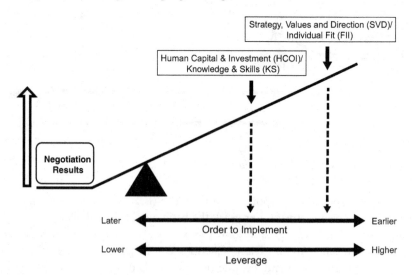

Figure 3.6 Leveraging HCOI and KS for Results

Finally, after SVD/IF and HCOI/KS have been implemented and aligned, the last piece of the puzzle is Organizational Incentives, followed by Individual Interests. OI on its own will certainly have an impact but rarely one that will sustain the organization. That said, OI can be powerful when directly aligned with and supporting both SVD and HCOI, which is why it must be done after the first two. In addition, it must be done well—time must be taken to design and align incentives both with the strategy of the organization and with its linked individual competency of II. OI and II are the final pieces of the puzzle.

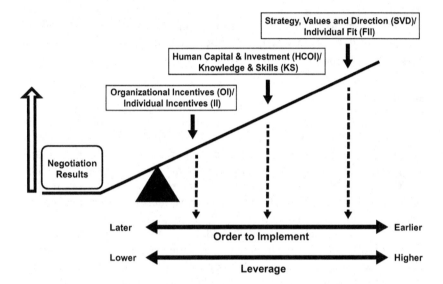

Figure 3.7 Leveraging OI and II for Results

To illustrate, consider a Fortune 100 company that finds itself struggling to retain its core of talented employees. They respond, at first, by funding a number of salary increases and expanding bonus structures. Unfortunately, this unilateral investment focused on monetary incentives did little to slow the talent drain from the company. It wasn't until they took a deeper approach to understand II and OI in tandem that they began to uncover the interests causing people to leave. Employees wanted to feel more closely connected to the core mission of the organization that was such a selling point in attracting talent in the first place. Individuals wanted more flexibility in terms of hours and the ability to work remotely. They wanted a clearer career progression that was more predictable rather than having to network with senior executives to get promoted. In other words, they wanted a number of important interests addressed that had little to do with salary.

Much can go wrong when the OI cart is put before the strategy horse. For example, salespeople are often incentivized to, well, sell. Incentives in the form of commissions on sales and bonuses on client satisfaction are put in place. Operations, however, are directed to reduce costs per unit and maintain high product quality, with bonuses tied to cost and quality measures. If sales is then wildly successful, it will create a large book of orders. Operations, meanwhile, has been trimming staff in a bid to reduce unit costs and has slowed production to improve certain quality issues. The incentives created in these two different units will likely produce significantly unintended consequences—production will either be ordered to ramp up quickly by hiring new staff or will be told to reduce quality targets (which they will likely resist to avoid missing their metrics and bonus); alternatively, sales will be told to try and keep customers on the string for a longer delivery time than promised, likely causing them to be less than honest with their customers to preserve their commissions. In either case, staff will be frustrated or disengaged when one or both feel thwarted by the lack of an integrated strategy and direction for the business.

Summary

To achieve sustained excellence in negotiation, each step of the negotiation process must be engineered and sequenced effectively. So far, we've seen at a high level how the NCM addresses all areas of the negotiation process and the specific sequencing of each of these areas that will be most effective. The NCM and its foundation in behavioral engineering provide a road map for building, step by step, the capabilities to achieve success in every negotiation the organization needs to have.

In the next three chapters, we'll go deeper into each of the capabilities and start looking at the specific activities and the key practices that will build this foundation. After that, we will go even deeper into the implementation process and present two specific approaches, two "journey maps," that will help guide any organization planning to dramatically improve their negotiation function.

Notes

1 Gilbert, T. F. (2007). *Human competence: Engineering worthy behaviour.* Pfeiffer.
2 www.npr.org/2021/11/29/1059821677/google-dont-be-evil-lawsuit
3 www.npr.org/2021/09/10/1035901596/harvard-university-end-investment-fossil-fuel-industry-climate-change-activism
4 Adapted from Updating the Behaviour Engineering Model, Roger Chevalier, ISPI 2003.

4   Level 2 NCM—Repeatable Competency

Introduction

In Chapter 1, we introduced the Negotiation Assessment Tool (NAT), the diagnostic instrument which identified the common state of Ad Hockery within the Negotiation Capability Model (NCM), where negotiation practices tended to be unplanned and reactive. Also, we identified three progressive levels in the NCM of negotiation capability that started with Level 2: Repeatable Competency, moved up to Level 3: Adaptive Flexibility, and aspired to Level 4: Optimized Performance in the negotiation function. In Chapter 3, we introduced the NCM itself, which identified six core areas of negotiation capability—three organizational and three individual—and explained how these aligned into three pairs of capabilities as a framework for building the capacity that leads to negotiation success.

In this chapter, we will explore the second level from the NCM—Repeatable Competency—and lay out a pathway toward building this as a foundation for ongoing negotiation success in any organizational context.

Repeatability

Repeatability is the critical first step in creating any change that can be sustained. Without repeatability, any endeavor or any system is simply random and unpredictable—anything can happen (and usually does!). Ad Hockery is characterized by improvisation based on impulse and reaction—by starting to prepare for a negotiation the night before, for example. Information and data are gathered from the nearest and easiest sources—colleagues and friends—rather than appropriate sources. At the table, negotiators play it by ear, react in the moment rather than execute a plan and strategy. When organizations allow these widely divergent and random approaches to any issue or problem, the results, not surprisingly, are also random and divergent. Sustained change or improvement of any kind requires, as a first step, that a repeatable process is identified and implemented. This is, essentially, the price of admission.

The examples for a repeatable approach are endless. If you want to improve physical fitness, exercise must be planned and performed regularly

DOI:10.4324/9781003243854-5

based on the desired goals and outcomes. If a runner wants to finish a marathon within a certain time, a training plan with that specific goal in mind is needed. Anyone, of course, can enter and show up to run a race. Without a repeatable training plan, individual results will be random—many will drop out, some might finish, a few might even do well. It is well known, however, that just about anyone can finish a marathon if they train by following a plan, by building their capacity, by executing a training schedule. Anyone can become a competent runner simply by training—systematically and repeatedly.

In the business world, McDonald's rose to the highest levels of the fast-food industry by building repeatable plans for every single function in the restaurant. They regularly take teenagers, a demographic that has little life experience and less natural inclination toward discipline, and through a training process based on specific and repeatable actions and skills, develop competence and excellence every day. They are masters at creating Repeatable Competency.

It is no different, in principle, for building negotiation excellence. The first step is to create repeatable processes based on core competencies specific to negotiation.

Repeatable Competencies in Negotiation

The negotiation process has its own framework for building Repeatable Competency (a framework that is quite different from McDonald's, by the way). At a minimum, Repeatable Competency in the negotiation function must include:

- **Recognition of negotiation as a necessary organizational competency.** The starting point is the recognition that negotiation is indeed a core competency of the organization. If it is seen as simply a small part of an individual's performance appraisal, a sideline task to the main part of their job, or as being too complex to address, the organization will be reliant on unpredictable (i.e., random) outcomes after the fact.
- **Purposeful practice—a systemic approach.** Negotiation, like training for a marathon, must have a structured approach to preparation; it must have a plan for what happens face-to-face at the table; and it must have clear goals to measure success. Negotiation must not simply follow the individual preferences of each person negotiating, it must have a process and framework that everyone follows. This framework can certainly have a small amount of latitude for individual preferences, but the system, as a system, must be followed by all.
- **Organizational values.** A critical part of any repeatable approach to negotiation is ensuring that the values of the organization are embedded in every step of the process to ensure that all results achieved align with these values.

- **Embedding a cultural approach to negotiation.** Culture can be defined as simply "The way we do things around here." Culture is a series of deeply embedded values, actions, and activities that are part of the fabric of the organization. Designing and embedding the organization's values along with a systemic approach to each and every negotiation creates a strong negotiation culture that leads to success, over and over.

- **Organizational interests.** In addition to core values, strategic goals and objectives (long-term and short-term) need to be identified, assessed, and then embedded in the negotiation process. Without this, negotiations gravitate to negotiators simply trying to "get as much as they can," or "get the best price," rather than achieving specific strategic goals that help ensure the success of the business.

- **Training.** For repeatable results that align with organizational values, strategies, and goals, training for negotiators must be designed and implemented in a way that is tailored to the specific needs of the organization. In addition, the skills and tools learned need to actually be implemented and put directly into practice. Sending staff to take generic negotiation training typically results in inconsistent application at best or zero application back in the workplace at worst.

- **Measurement.** The hallmark of repeatability is measurement and feedback. The only way that continuous improvement of any activity is achieved is when systematic and repeatable actions take place, the results from these are measured, and the measurements are fed back in a way that changes and improves the system. The results of changes are also measured, fed back, with further changes and improvements. And so on. Many years of research and testing of quality control systems have demonstrated the value of this approach over and over. Through ongoing cycles of measurement and feedback, long-term success can be built, step by step.

Everything described earlier starts with the implementation of proven practices in a repeatable and measurable way. Level 2: Repeatable Competency is the starting point.

Looking at the negotiation process, what are these Repeatable Competencies? Negotiation is a complex and subtle human process, far more nuanced than producing perfect french fries each and every time. To understand Level 2 repeatability in the negotiation process, we have broken the process into the six areas as identified by the NCM. We'll explore each of them in the following.

The NCM—Level 2 Repeatable Competency

As we saw in Chapter 3, there are three specific areas of organizational competence, three key performance areas (KPAs) at the organizational level, and these three areas are paired and aligned with three KPAs of individual competence. These areas were described at a high level and now need to be refined and crystallized into activities and practices that can be understood and implemented.

As will be detailed in Chapter 7: Mapping the Journey, we start in each case with the organizational key practice, then move to the individual practice it is aligned with, both of them focused on creating a foundation of repeatable and predictable practices at both levels that will lead to long-term results.

KPA #1: Strategy, Values, and Direction (SVD)

The purpose of the SVD key performance area for Level 2 is to ensure the organization has established clear values that are fully embedded within a focused strategy. This strategy and direction must be a part of all negotiation activities that take place within the organization. The SVD key performance area is directly aligned with the Individual Fit (IF) KPA.

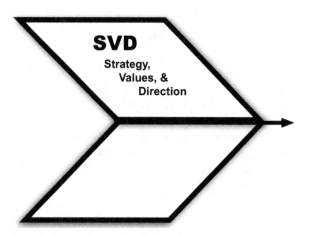

Figure 4.1 Strategy, Values, and Direction KPA—Level 2

In specific, the goal of the SVD key performance area at Level 2 is to ensure that the organization builds and repeatedly employs these specific competencies:

- Organizational values are embedded in negotiation strategy, goals, and objectives;
- Negotiation is seen and treated as an organizational competency;
- Negotiation goals and objectives are clearly defined;
- A clear negotiation culture is established to ensure a common language and behavioral norms;

- A measurement framework is in place to evaluate negotiation performance at all levels;
- The organization's strategy and values are embedded in all negotiation training programs.

Key Capabilities and Key Practices—SVD

At the end of the day, negotiation is a practical activity conducted frequently in a wide range of areas in our organizations. This means that any framework for negotiations, any approach that theoretically will result in better outcomes, must be grounded in specific activities, behaviors and practices that can be implemented and measured. In Chapter 3 we looked at the higher-level concepts of SVD that make it necessary to address. The next step for each performance area, therefore, is to implement tangible activities, Key Practices (KPs), that are grounded in the specific capabilities the organization is developing.

For SVD, the following capabilities must be identified as necessary for the negotiation function, followed by implementation of KPs that deliver on those capabilities.

1. **Ability to communicate and reinforce organizational values in all negotiations.**

   Organizational values are key success drivers for an organization across a wide range of activities, and negotiation is no different. Inherent in the concept of business and the proverbial marketplace is the idea of delivering services efficiently, making money, or generating profit. In a free market, it's also clear that organizations produce revenue through some form of competition. In the private sector, it's a straight line from profit to success. In nonprofit organizations—government, social service organizations, charities—profit isn't the driver, but money itself becomes even more important—lowering costs, reducing spending, delivering better services, and increasing revenue through grants, donations, or taxes. Consciously and unconsciously, employees at all levels focus on these important concerns. The risk, however, is that monetary concerns become paramount, or even become the exclusive focus, often eclipsing far more important values for the organization.

   In the late 1990s, it was common for cigarette companies to donate money to a wide array of organizations—charities helping with homelessness, community organizations, even healthcare in inner cities. Many organizations, just grateful to have the resources, accepted. Even earlier, many universities had endowments that invested in companies based or doing business in South Africa, essentially profiting from apartheid to increase their returns. Clearly, little attention at the time was paid to aligning their broader values with these investment decisions; organizations focused solely on the monetary benefit, as if the monetary benefit was the only outcome of importance. This misalignment of values eventually started to be noticed, and many people objected. Shareholders rebelled at annual general meetings, boycotts of companies were organized, students at universities demonstrated. The result was a great deal of conflict, internally and externally, as this clash of values was played out. In the end, many organizations got the message and changed, but only after intense and costly battles. When values are not aligned with the negotiation and decision-making process, a great deal of time, energy, and money can be spent, along with lasting damage to reputations and important relationships.

A critical capability for every organization, therefore, is its ability to communicate and reinforce its values to help guide the negotiation process at all times.

SVD Key Practice #1: Core organizational and negotiation values are explicitly identified as part of a strategic plan that is current and well publicized.

- Every successful organization has a strategic plan, but few specifically identify the core values it expects in the organization's negotiation activities. Negotiation is a high-profile demonstration of every organization's values, and by having the organization's core values for negotiation identified and routinely communicated to its negotiation staff, results aligned with those values will be delivered.

2. **Ability to establish and practice strategic planning around all negotiations.**
   After clarity around values, strategic planning for each negotiation is the next capability that needs to be developed. Strategy in negotiation identifies, from a wide range of goals, which goals are the most important to achieve. Without a requirement to have strategic conversations before every negotiation (appropriate to the size and importance of each negotiation, of course), the unconscious bias of simply serving our immediate and short-term interests takes over. Negotiation-competent organizations make sure every negotiation has a clear, simple, and strategic focus before going to the table.

   SVD Key Practice #2: Every negotiation is required to have a clear, if simple, strategy—in writing.

   - Strategy need not be complex or even elaborate. A plan that aligns with the organization's broader strategy and values, appropriate to the size and complexity of the negotiation, is in place and is reviewed prior to the start of bargaining.

3. **Ability to develop and implement specific procedures, practices, roles and responsibilities that define and guide the negotiation process.**
   One of the major signs of Ad Hockery is that each negotiation is run differently, with different processes for preparation, different practices

for data gathering, and a lack of clarity regarding roles and responsibilities. These differences are often based on the personal preferences of different negotiation leaders. By establishing common and repeatable practices along with clear roles and responsibilities, the organization creates the foundation for Repeatable Competency.

SVD Key Practice #3A: Specific negotiation processes and procedures are established.

• Simple but standard processes and steps for preparation, data gathering, and pre-negotiation discussions are in place, along with a process for confirming strategy and values, for every negotiation. This creates a predictable, repeatable, and robust negotiation process each and every time.

SVD Key Practice #3B: Roles and responsibilities for all negotiations processes are established and communicated.

• Establishing role clarity and defining who does what on each negotiation allows all staff to focus on high-value activities.

4. **Ability to integrate measurement and KPIs as a critical part of the negotiation process, along with an ability to review, assess, and learn from each negotiation to ensure continuous organizational learning and development.**
   Negotiated outcomes are often hard to assess—was the negotiation successful? How do we know? Did we achieve what we needed? More importantly, is the outcome aligned with our values and strategy? Negotiation outcomes are the result of many moving parts, such as market conditions, behavior of competitors, the financial state of ourselves and the party we are negotiating with, internal priorities, time, and timing. It can be difficult to link any given negotiated outcome with the actions we took before and during the negotiation. This fact is often used as an excuse to not bother trying.

   This is a mistake. Negotiation as a process is like any other system or process an organization runs—it can be measured and improved on an ongoing basis. The starting point for linking outcomes with effective negotiation processes is measurement.

   As with most business processes, we don't want to measure indiscriminately or try to measure everything. Repeatable Competency requires that we carefully target a minimum number of KPIs and track them regularly. These KPIs might include measures of preparation time spent, length of negotiation, target outcomes compared to actual outcomes, market data comparisons, relationship status, and so on. Once measurements are established, they can ensure proper resourcing of the negotiation function, along with supporting a strong debrief and learning process after each negotiation.

SVD Key Practice #4A: A measurement and evaluation plan that tracks the successes and setbacks of the negotiation program is in place.

- The organization identifies what is measured and evaluated, allowing regular assessment of the negotiation process itself and linking that information to reasons for both successes and setbacks at the bargaining table.

SVD Key Practice #4B: Basic scorecard and other simple KPIs are established for negotiation activities.

- Measurements are refined down to a set of KPIs on a simple scorecard or dashboard, allowing the organization to know exactly how the negotiation function is performing quickly and easily.

SVD Key Practice #4C: A peer review process is in place for negotiation planning, strategy, and evaluation.

- Negotiation is often treated as a unique and specialized silo, with each person who has a negotiation function operating in their own little bubble. Building a strong peer review forum that brings everyone in the negotiation function together regularly to review best practices around planning, strategy, execution, and evaluation creates a powerful learning function within the organization.

Summary—Strategy, Values, and Direction

A key goal of the SVD performance area is to set the high-level expectations and overall strategy for the negotiation function. It is only at the organizational level that these goals can be established, along with the expectation that individual activity and behavior will align with the expectations that SVD establishes. This alignment leads us to the individual KPA that is directly linked to SVD, Individual Fit.

KPA #2: Individual Fit (IF)

The purpose of the IF key performance area for Level 2 is to ensure that all individuals working in the negotiation space in the organization are fully aligned with the SVD of the organization. It is well known that many organizations have beautifully crafted mission and vision statements hanging on their walls, and nothing but lip service is paid. This does not, in any way, mean that mission and vision statements are a waste of time—they are not. But they are useful only if the values and direction they embody are implemented by the people in the organization. By focusing on this alignment with negotiation staff and crystallizing the individual key practices that demonstrate this alignment, the organization's strategy and values can be directly put into action. The IF key performance area is directly aligned with the KPA of organizational SVD.

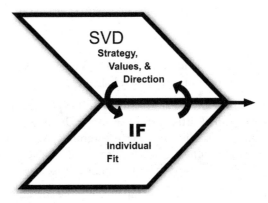

Figure 4.2 Individual Fit KPA—Level 2

The goal of the IF key practice area at Level 2 is meant to ensure the individuals responsible for negotiation activities build and employ these specific competencies:

- Individual values are aligned with the organization's negotiation strategy, goals, and values
- Individuals understand and are committed to the philosophy and culture of the organization
- Individuals understand and are committed to the negotiation practices and frameworks established by the organization
- Individuals demonstrate continuous learning and self-reflection as ongoing competencies
- Individuals are committed to measurement and evaluation of negotiation processes and outcomes

Key Capabilities and Key Practices—IF

For the SVD of the organization to be brought directly into each and every negotiation, each individual negotiator's values and behaviors must be a fit with the organization. Each individual must be willing and able to demonstrate this fit throughout the negotiation process. The following are the individuals' key practices that demonstrate alignment with the SVD of the organization.

1. **Ability to communicate and reinforce organizational values in all negotiations.**
   Organizational values are not, and should never be, a secret. Effective negotiators should communicate organizational values throughout the negotiation process and use them as a factor in decisions made in the negotiation process.

IF Key Practice #1: Individuals regularly establish and communicate organizational values during negotiations, both internally and across the table.

- By routinely discussing and demonstrating organizational values within the negotiation process, values become a lived part of every negotiation that indicates individual alignment.

2. **Ability to follow and execute the specific procedures, practices, roles, and responsibilities established for the negotiation process.**
   Demonstrating the ability to apply a systemic approach to all negotiations is the cornerstone of moving from Ad Hockery to Repeatable Competency. This leads to the following key practices:

   IF Key Practice #2A: Individuals apply the strategic planning process in every negotiation.

   - Every negotiation is viewed as fitting into a broader strategic plan and has clear strategic goals in place.

   IF Key Practice #2B: Individuals follow specific procedures and practices based on clear roles and responsibilities for every negotiation.

   - The negotiation process, from start to finish, is mapped out and executed as planned. Negotiation should never be a process of "winging it" in the moment, and only by having a clear framework ahead of time will the negotiation process regularly go in the direction that is needed. While the ability to be flexible and adapt to new information is also necessary, these changes will still be guided by the overall goals and objectives that are established in the planning phase.

3. **Ability to measure and track key performance indicators (KPIs) as an ongoing and critical part of the negotiation process.**
   Negotiators must see measurements and KPIs not as a secondary activity to do only if there's time but as an integral part of the negotiation process, one that gives both real time and long-term feedback to ensure repeatable success at the table. To achieve this, the key practices include:

   IF Key Practice #3: Negotiators identify, track, and use measurements and KPIs as an integral part of their negotiation process.

   - Measurements need to be simple and relevant, with each measurement adding value to the process. Negotiators must demonstrate their ongoing commitment to the use of metrics as a key practice.

4. **Ability to approach each negotiation from an integrative perspective, with an ability to engage successfully on distributive issues as needed.**
   As previously noted, an integrative approach tends to meet far more interests of both parties than a distributive approach. That said, some

issues require a more distributive approach, and negotiators must be able to maintain and build relationships with other parties in either situation.

IF Key Practice #4A: Every negotiation is framed and planned from an integrative perspective.

IF Key Practice #4B: When distributive issues arise, negotiators are comfortable being firm in meeting organizational interests while maintaining organizational values and relationships with negotiating partners at the same time.

5. **Ability to review, assess, and learn from each negotiation to ensure continuous learning and self-improvement.**
   Continuous learning, in any field, is the only way to incrementally improve results. Negotiation is no different. Each individual must be committed to reviewing, assessing, and learning from every negotiation to stay aligned with organizational values and strategy.

   IF Key Practice #5: Negotiators debrief every negotiation with a focus on self-reflection and continuous individual improvement.

   • Reflective practice is a must for negotiators who work in one of the most complex and fluid areas of human interaction.

Summary—Individual Fit

Overall, the goal of the IF KPA is simple—it's to ensure that all individuals working in the negotiation arena fit within the organization's SVD. Broadly speaking, this is the most foundational area where alignment is needed to produce long-term success at the table.

KPA #3: Human Capital and Organizational Investment (HCOI)

The purpose of the HCOI key performance area for Level 2 is to ensure the organization has identified and developed specific negotiation-focused policies, procedures, and practices that align with organizational strategy, and has committed to investing in hiring, training, and supporting the negotiation function across the organization. HCOI is directly linked to the individual Knowledge and Skills (KS) key performance area.

More specifically, the goals of the HCOI key practice area for Level 2 is to ensure the organization invests the necessary time and resources into these competencies:

• Strategies for hiring negotiation staff are aligned with organizational values
• Human resources policies, procedures, and practices to support and retain negotiators are in place

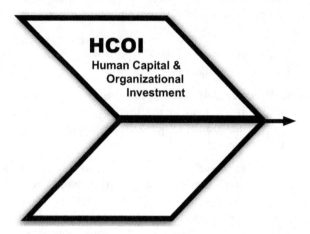

Figure 4.3 Human Capital and Organizational Investment KPA—Level 2

- Time, tools, training, and materials to deliver negotiation results are identified and provided
- Organizational investment in negotiation infrastructure is budgeted for and supports the ongoing development of all negotiation competencies

Key Capabilities and Practices—HCOI

The human resource function is often seen as "soft," meaning it is difficult to measure objectively. This is especially true in the negotiation arena, where the simplest approach is to focus solely on tangible results, outcomes from each negotiation, and ignore all the activities and behaviors that create those results. We cannot control results; what we can control are our activities and behaviors that produce results. Without a strong framework of activities and practices that all negotiators operate within, without clear expectations on how negotiations will be conducted, and without investment that supports these expectations, entropy will again take over, with each negotiator simply doing what is most comfortable for them. The organization will suffer.

For HCOI, the following capabilities must be identified as necessary for the negotiation function, followed by implementation of key practices that deliver on those capabilities.

1. **Ability to hire negotiation staff who are aligned with organizational values.**
   Hiring tends to focus primarily on skill and experience. While these are important, they should be secondary to assessing the values and beliefs about the negotiation process that potential candidates bring with them. If a candidate sees their role as being left alone to deliver

results, they simply won't fit well into a structured approach to negotiation. The hiring process must be designed to evaluate each candidate's overall approach to negotiation as part of the process.

HCOI Key Practice #1: Hiring criteria are based on assessing candidate values and negotiation approaches first and foremost.

- With the help of experienced hiring firms or a strong in-house human resources function, the hiring process is revised to ensure each potential candidate's core values around the negotiating function are aligned before being hired. Negotiating skill and experience are assessed after values are aligned.

2. **Ability to provide human resource processes that directly support the negotiation function.**
   Specific policies and procedures from a human resource perspective must be in place to ensure the negotiation function is supported. This may include:

   HCOI Key Practice #2A: A performance and evaluation process specific to the negotiation function is developed and applied.

   - Negotiators should get job-relevant feedback on performance regularly.

   HCOI Key Practice #2B: A clear career progression and promotion process is established for negotiation staff.

   - Often, the negotiation skill set is seen as applicable only to negotiating contracts, leading to a dead end for many skilled negotiators. The organization should establish and communicate a full career path for the negotiation function to ensure talent is retained and well utilized. This may include an array of roles where these skills are critical—even if not a primary function of that role.

   HCOI Key Practice #2C: Negotiation activities and successes are recognized and acknowledged.

   - When negotiation is essentially an ad hoc activity, it becomes difficult to acknowledge success. A few "big wins" can seem to be obvious but recognizing only results reinforces the win-lose mentality for negotiation. Acknowledgment for applying a systemic approach to negotiation and for upholding organizational values in every negotiation should be regularly recognized to build the long-term culture that Repeatable Competency brings.

3. **Ability to invest resources effectively across the negotiation function.**
   The organization must choose to allocate and invest in a full range of activities that comprise the negotiation function. These key practices include:

   HCOI Key Practice #3A: Budgets are allocated to provide time and resources for effective preparation, research, and planning prior to engaging in negotiations.

- In all negotiations, preparation is critical. Time to plan, gather information, and prepare effectively is identified, provided, and encouraged.

HCOI Key Practice #3B: Training that aligns with organizational values and goals is provided on an ongoing basis and is designed around evidence-based negotiation theory.

- Training cannot be done generically or as a series of one-off events. Training must integrate directly into the specific negotiation function for each organization. Finally, all training should be validated around evidence-based negotiation theory, not the many "pop-culture" fads that periodically sweep through the field.

HCOI Key Practice #3C: Mentoring and/or learning forums are provided and integrated into the ongoing negotiation function.

- Formal or structured training, while necessary, rarely helps people translate what has been learned directly into practice. Individual mentoring and peer learning forums are aimed at supporting negotiators to implement specific approaches and skills, ensuring that training translates into practice.

4. **Ability to establish and communicate clear roles and responsibilities for all negotiation functions.**
   Role clarity is a necessary precursor to success in any organizational context, and negotiation is no different. Establishing clear roles allows for full accountability for results.

   HCOI Key Practice #4: Documentation through role descriptions is in place to clarify expectations across the negotiation function.

5. **Ability to provide negotiators with software and databases to collect, assess, and evaluate data and KPIs effectively.**
   Measurements are useful only if the data is captured in an accessible and useful way.

   HCOI Key Practice #5: Activity-based metrics and the software and tools to use them effectively are made available and supported.

Summary—Human Capital and Organizational Investment

The Human Capital and Organizational Investment performance area takes higher-level SVD and puts it into practice by creating a range of policies and frameworks that support success. These frameworks must then be accepted and leveraged by staff to achieve results through the next key performance area, Knowledge and Skills.

KPA #4: Knowledge and Skills (KS)

The purpose of the Knowledge and Skills KPA for Level 2 is to ensure that all individuals with negotiation responsibilities make use of the time, tools, and training they have been provided through HCOI. In addition, it is to ensure that individuals reflect on and learn from their activities on an ongoing basis. Knowledge and Skills are directly aligned with the HCOI key performance area.

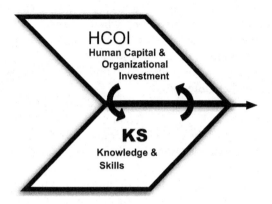

Figure 4.4 Knowledge and Skills KPA—Level 2

The goal of the Knowledge and Skills KPA at Level 2 is to ensure that all individuals responsible for negotiation activities:

- Participate in comprehensive training that teaches negotiation competencies aligned with strategy and values
- Engage fully with mentors and peers to assist with implementing and applying negotiation skills and competencies
- Routinely apply the established negotiation practices, policies, and procedures
- Give regular feedback to the organization to identify where investment and support is needed and regularly suggest improvements to negotiation procedures and practices

Key Capabilities and Key Practices—Knowledge and Skills

Knowledge and Skills for the individual is where repeatable practice will unfold. The following are the key practices for individuals that demonstrate alignment with the HCOI performance area of the organization.

1. **Ability to apply a wide range of negotiation knowledge, skills, and competencies when negotiating.**
   The outcome of effective training is the application of KS in the field.

   KS Key Practice #1A: Individuals attend high-quality training provided on a regular basis.

KS Key Practice #1B: Individuals can demonstrate the following core skills, at a minimum, on an ongoing basis:

- Understand common negotiation styles and frames:
  - o   Consistently recognize and apply core elements of integrative negotiation/value creation in most situations
  - o   Consistently recognize and apply core elements of distributive negotiation/value claiming when required
- Understand key variables in assessing negotiation power/strength and use this in developing negotiation strategy
- Consistently identify all parties' interests and tests assumptions related to these interests
- Consistently discover other parties' targets, resistance points, motives, and feelings of confidence
- Consistently apply basic engagement skills such as questioning, listening, acknowledging, and information gathering during the negotiation process:
  - o   Able to create a free flow of information in negotiation
- Understand their own side's BATNAs and WATNAs
  - o   Consistently work to understand the other side's BATNAs and WATNAs
- Consistently seek to improve negotiated agreements for all parties prior to finalizing any negotiation

2. **Ability to continuously develop and enhance personal negotiation skills.**
   Continuous improvement starts as a personal value and is demonstrated as follows:

   KS Key Practice #2A: Individuals engage in post-negotiation audits with a view to identifying areas for individual learning and improvement.

   KS Key Practice #2B: Individuals engage with mentors and peers in structured activities designed to identify areas for learning and improvement.

3. **Ability to execute the negotiation best practices and procedures established for the negotiation process.**
   The very essence of Repeatable Competency is that the negotiation process follows a similar process each and every time. Repeatable processes can then be measured and linked to success or failure, which in turn leads to rapid improvement.

   KS Key Practice #3: Individuals follow the established steps and processes for each negotiation.

4. **Ability to give regular feedback on continuous improvement ideas based on information from measurements and KPIs.**

With the organization collecting ongoing KPI and measurement information, negotiators must use this information for identifying areas where the practices and processes can be improved based on this information.

KS #4: Negotiators give regular feedback and ideas for improvement of the negotiation process itself.

- Once data is available and patterns emerge, it is up to the frontline negotiators to identify areas for ongoing improvement of the negotiation process. These suggestions must be based on measurements and KPIs, not individual preference.

Summary—Knowledge and Skills

Knowledge and Skills are the bread and butter of success for negotiators. Once the organization has provided clear strategy and direction, and once the investment in human capital including time, tools, and training is made, it is up to each individual to develop their knowledge and skills to a high, and repeatable, level. After Knowledge and Skills, the final piece of the puzzle is to then consider the alignment of incentives and interests.

KPA #5: Organizational Incentives (OI)

The purpose of the Organizational Incentives KPA for Level 2 is to ensure the organization has designed, created, and assessed effective incentives for negotiation staff that directly align with the SVD of the organization. Frequently, organizations implement incentives that have unintended consequences, at times incentivizing the exact opposite of the outcomes that are being sought. Some incentives, such as bonuses or pay for performance schemes, create monetary incentives to promote certain behaviors. There can be many nonmonetary incentives as well, from recognition to promotions to perks such as support staff help or even choice of offices. OI is directly linked to the Individual Interests (II) key performance area.

The goal of the Organizational Incentives KPA, specifically for Level 2, is to ensure organizational incentives are in full alignment with the negotiation function:

- Incentives, both monetary and nonmonetary, are aligned with negotiation strategy and values;
- Measurements of negotiation practices and outcomes are aligned with monetary and nonmonetary incentives;
- Career progressions for negotiation staff are in place;
- Special attention is paid to internal relationships;
- Both short-term and long-term impacts are considered when creating incentive programs.

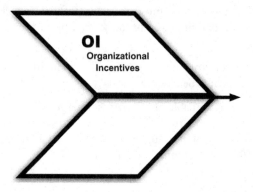

Figure 4.5 Organizational Incentives KPA—Level 2

Key Capabilities and Practices—OI

Organizations should develop clear and direct practices around incentives. For OI, the following capabilities and practices around incentives need to be considered, followed by implementation of key practices that deliver on those capabilities.

1. **Ability to strategically design both monetary and nonmonetary incentives that meet organizational interests.**
   As mentioned, incentives and disincentives exist in every function in every organization, whether done consciously or not. A full assessment of the incentives in the negotiation function, both real and perceived, should be undertaken. Incentives should be designed and implemented consciously.

   OI Key Practice #1A: Incentive programs are assessed, designed, and implemented to ensure individual negotiator behavior supports organizational values and goals.

   OI Key Practice #1B: Individual interests of negotiation staff are surveyed and understood regularly.

2. **Ability to measure and monitor the ongoing impact of organizational incentives.**
   What is an effective incentive today may well fade over time or worse, become a disincentive in the future.

   OI Key Practice #2: Incentive programs have metrics that ensure they remain effective or are revised to retain their effectiveness.

3. **Ability to engage staff around career progressions and succession planning.**
   Career planning and advancement are powerful incentives but only if they remain relevant.

OI Key Practice #3A: Career paths are developed interactively with staff wherever possible and are defined and communicated to staff regularly.

OI Key Practice #3B: Relationships with high-value staff are built and sustained over time.

Summary—Organizational Incentives

While this organizational KPA is narrower in scope than SVD and HCOI, it is quite influential. Structural incentives are powerful influencers. If negotiation staff see incentives that run against the SVD of the organization, the incentives usually win. One of the most powerful incentives for each individual is their own personal interests, which is why OI is directly linked to the Individual Interests key performance area.

KPA #6: Individual Interests (II)

The purpose of the Individual Interests KPA is to ensure that the individual interests of negotiation staff are identified and aligned with the interests of the organization. The II KPA makes sure that individuals make known their interests and give feedback regularly on the alignment between organizational incentives and individual interests. Individual Interests are directly linked to the OI key performance area.

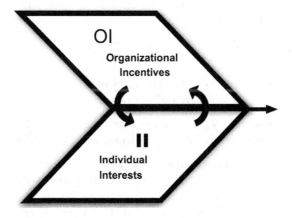

Figure 4.6 Individual Interests KPA—Level 2

The goal of the Individual Interests KPA, specifically for Level 2, is to ensure that Individual Interests are known and understood and remain in alignment with Organizational Incentives.

- Individual interests and goals, both monetary and nonmonetary, are fully aligned with the organization's interests and goals throughout the negotiation process and beyond

- Negotiation staffs' interests and motives are surveyed and understood regularly
- Individuals identify where individual interests appear misaligned with organizational interests
- Individuals focus on building strong internal relationships

Key Capabilities and Key Practices—II

Individual interests are the strongest motivators that exist—in fact, the only true motivator for every person is their assessment of their own individual interests. What each one of us wants, needs, hopes for, or is concerned about directs our behavior every waking moment. When we look at interests within the negotiation process, behavior at the table is driven by the stated, unstated, and ever-changing assessment of interests by each party as they work toward an agreement.

The starting point for an organization to be effective at the bargaining table is that their negotiators' interests and motives are fully aligned with the organization's interests before they get anywhere near leading a negotiation. Each individual needs to be able to share information about their interests regularly. The Individual Interests KPA is designed to bring this forward and address it.

1. **Ability to communicate long- and short-term goals and interests directly to the organization.**
   Individuals must ensure that the organization knows and understands their interests and goals.

   II Key Practice #1: Individual input is regularly given, and organizational incentives are kept in broad alignment.

2. **Ability to identify misalignments quickly and clearly.**
   Individuals must see a clear and safe process where they can be heard.

   II Key Practice #2: Individuals commit to quickly raising misalignment issues and mixed-motive problems through agreed processes.

3. **Ability to build and maintain strong organizational relationships.**
   Individual interests can sometimes obscure negotiators from seeing the interests of the people around them, be they support staff or other areas of the organization. Strong internal relationships help ensure that individual interests are seen more broadly, reinforcing a culture of success.

   II Key Practice #3: Individuals reach out and build cross-functional relationships across the organization wherever appropriate.

Summary—Individual Interests

While the organization needs to be skilled at engaging staff to understand their interests, staff themselves have an obligation to share that information as well. The Individual Interests KPA creates a two-way street that keeps these interests in full alignment.

Summary—Negotiation Capability Model at Level 2

When the systems, processes, and structures begin to align, when what seems like the simple act of negotiating is underpinned in these areas, it allows negotiators to fully engage and focus on achieving outcomes that benefit everyone in the value chain. When friction from internal lack of clarity disappears, when effective preparation becomes the norm instead of the exception, negotiated outcomes will routinely support and drive success for the whole organization.

Level 2, remember, is both a destination and a starting point. Achieving Level 2: Repeatable Competency is a destination, in that having repeatable processes that deliver on the needs of the organization will put your organization in the top 20–25% of organizations nationwide. Or worldwide, for that matter. It will create that foundation for effective negotiations now and in the future.

It is also a starting point, in that there are two additional and higher levels of achievement; in this context, Level 2 can be seen as simply a steppingstone. The next level is Level 3: Adaptive Flexibility, where the organization can expand its current best practices from simple competence to being adaptable, flexible, and nimble—all while maintaining a strong foundation of repeatability. Level 3: Adaptive Flexibility is the subject of the next chapter. There, we'll show you how this foundation of Level 2 can be expanded and extended from basic competence to a higher level of mastery in the negotiation function.

Key Practices Condensed—Level 2: Repeatable Competency

In summary, to achieve Level 2, the Key Practices at this level are captured here—at a minimum, Level 2 Key Practices must include the following:

Strategy, Values, and Direction:

SVD #1: Core organizational and negotiation values are explicitly identified as part of a strategic plan that is current and well publicized.

SVD #2: Every negotiation is required to have a clear, if simple, strategy in writing.

SVD #3A: Specific negotiation process and procedures are established.

SVD #3B: Roles and responsibilities for all negotiations are established and communicated.

SVD #4A: A measurement and evaluation plan that measures the successes and setbacks of the negotiation program is in place.

SVD #4B: Basic scorecard and other simple KPIs are established for negotiation activities.

SVD #4C: A peer review process is in place for negotiation planning, strategy, and evaluation.

Individual Fit:

IF #1: Individuals regularly establish and communicate organizational values during negotiations, both internally and across the table.

IF #2A: Individuals apply the strategic planning process in every negotiation.

IF #2B: Individuals follow specific procedures and practices based on clear roles and responsibilities for every negotiation.

IF #3: Negotiators identify, track, and use measurements and KPIs as an integral part of their negotiation process.

IF #4A: Every negotiation is framed and planned from an integrative perspective.

IF #4B: When distributive issues arise, negotiators are comfortable being firm in meeting organizational interests while maintaining organizational values and relationships with negotiating partners at the same time.

IF #5: Negotiators debrief every negotiation with a focus on self-reflection and continuous individual improvement.

Human Capital and Organizational Investment:

HCOI #1: Hiring criteria is based on assessing candidate values and negotiation approaches first and foremost.

HCOI #2A: A basic performance and evaluation process specific to the negotiation function is developed and applied.

HCOI #2B: A clear career progression and promotion process is established for negotiation staff.

HCOI #2C: Negotiation activities and successes are recognized and acknowledged.

HCOI #3A: Budgets are allocated to provide time and resources for effective preparation, research, and planning prior to engaging in negotiations.

HCOI #3B: Training that aligns with organizational values and goals is provided on an ongoing basis and is designed around evidence-based negotiation theory.

HCOI #3C: Mentoring and/or learning forums are provided and integrated into the ongoing negotiation function.

HCOI #4: Documentation through role descriptions is in place to clarify expectations across the negotiation function.

HCOI Key Practice #5: Activity-based metrics, and the software and tools to use them effectively, are made available and supported.

Knowledge and Skills:

KS #1A: Individuals attend high-quality training provided on a regular basis.

KS #1B: Individuals are able to demonstrate the following core skills at a minimum on an ongoing basis:

- Understands common negotiation styles and frames
  - o Consistently recognizes core elements of distributive negotiation/value claiming situations
  - o Consistently recognizes core elements of integrative negotiation/value creating situations

- Understands key variables in assessing negotiation power/strength and uses this in developing negotiation strategy
- Consistently identifies all parties' interests and tests assumptions related to these interests
- Consistently discovers other parties' targets, resistance points, motives, and feelings of confidence
- Consistently applies basic engagement skills such as questioning, listening, acknowledging, and information gathering during the negotiation process
  - o Able to create a free flow of information in negotiation

- Understands their own side's BATNAs and WATNAs
  - o Consistently works to understand the other side's BATNAs and WATNAs

- Consistently seeks to improve negotiated agreements for all parties prior to finalizing any negotiation

KS #2A: Individuals engage in post-negotiation audits with a view to identifying areas for individual learning and improvement.

KS #2B: Individuals engage with mentors and peers in structured activities designed to identify areas for learning and improvement.

KS #3: Individuals follow the established steps and processes for each negotiation.

KS #4: Negotiators give regular feedback and ideas for improvement of the negotiation process itself.

Organizational Incentives:

OI #1A: Incentive programs are assessed, designed, and implemented to ensure individual negotiator behavior aligns with organization values and goals.

OI #1B: Individual interests of negotiation staff are surveyed and understood regularly.

OI #2: Incentive programs have metrics that ensure they remain effective or are revised to retain their effectiveness.

OI #3A: Career paths are developed interactively with staff wherever possible and are defined and communicated to staff regularly.

OI #3B: Relationships with high-value staff are built and sustained over time.

Individual Interests:

II #1: Individual input is regularly given, and organizational incentives are kept in broad alignment.

II #2: Individuals commit to raising misalignment issues and mixed-motive problems through agreed processes quickly.

II #3: Individuals reach out and build cross-functional relationships across the organization wherever appropriate.

5 Level 3 NCM—Adaptive Flexibility

Introduction

In Chapter 3, we established a systemic approach to the negotiation process, one that identified six areas of focus that will start the process of building simple, repeatable approaches to negotiation success. In Chapter 4, we explored Level 2: Repeatable Competency as the first level of a systemic approach to the negotiation process, looking at specific practices in each of the six areas of the NCM needed to build simple, repeatable approaches to negotiation success. Establishing a consistent level of practice that regularly delivers results is an achievement that can also be the final destination for the organization. Or Level 2 can also be seen as the precursor to helping the organization gain even better results by building greater adaptability and flexibility on the foundation that Level 2 has established.

In this chapter, we will explore the next level of the NCM identified by the Negotiation Assessment Tool—Level 3: Adaptive Flexibility—and describe the process of refining and enhancing the organizational and individual capabilities put in place at Level 2. These enhancements are designed to take the practice of negotiation from competence to artistry. From reading and playing a musical score to improvising jazz.

Adaptability

Moving from the Ad Hockery of Level 1 to the Repeatable Competency of Level 2 represents a major organizational milestone. Creating consistency by building true organizational competency in negotiation fundamentally transforms both the process and the outcomes around negotiation. So, it'd be understandable if there's a moment of pause when being asked to now reintroduce a degree of variability into the organization's negotiation practices—this time, however, on purpose, with the goal of adapting and improving quickly at the table. Quite importantly, the flexibility we are introducing at Level 3 is done with purpose, fundamentally different from the individual (and random) improvisation that created the Ad Hockery we saw in Level 1. With Level 3: Adaptive Flexibility, we are expanding our

DOI:10.4324/9781003243854-6

organizational skills and capabilities by varying our processes and practices for each unique negotiation as a way to deliver greater value. Exploring new approaches in a planned and purposeful way creates a process of continuous learning, continuous improvement, and rapid adaptation to new challenges.

The increased capabilities for Level 3: Adaptive Flexibility remain focused on the six areas of the NCM and are focused on the negotiation processes within the organization itself.

Adaptive Flexibility in Negotiation

Adaptive Flexibility extends the organization's negotiation framework by building on the repeatable practices introduced in the previous chapter. Once repeatable practices are in place, negotiators can begin to identify and create strategies and approaches tailored to the unique features of each negotiation. In culinary terms, Level 2 is akin to carefully following a recipe that consistently results in good-tasting food each time. Level 3 frees the chef to try new flavorings and enhancements that make the food surprising and memorable. It brings a full measure of creativity back, layering it on top of the repeatable foundation.

At a minimum, moving to the level of Adaptive Flexibility enhances the organization's negotiation function in a number of important ways:

- **Recognition that failing to evolve may be evolving to fail.** The move to Level 2: Repeatable Competency fixes many of the pain points felt around your organization's negotiation practices. It helps by creating a common culture with consistent practices. For some parts of your organization, this may be the full measure of development needed to succeed. That said, other areas of your organization might need to continually improve and evolve their negotiation capabilities, and these adaptations will likely look different across different functions in your organization. This growth and evolution will allow negotiation to consistently deliver value in different areas and with different strategies across the organization.
- **Systematize Adaptive Flexibility.** For your organization to remain nimble and remain on a path of continuous improvement, it must learn to effectively identify what is and isn't working, even with a strong foundation from Level 2. We started by systematizing processes in Level 2; we now need to systematize change itself at Level 3. By supporting flexibility within a systemic approach, organizational habits are created for rapidly adapting, evaluating, and adapting further.
- **Variation within a common set of values and goals.** To be clear, the importance of alignment between negotiation practices and organizational values remains at the forefront. Creativity and adaptability can, and must, remain closely aligned to the organization's SVD identified in Level 2.
- **Maintain a common culture with subcultures that align.** The need to create and maintain a common culture surrounding negotiation is critical. Once established, allowing and supporting subcultures

that meet local needs more effectively while remaining aligned with the overall culture is the next step.

- **Leverage organizational knowledge to a far deeper level.** The freedom to incorporate deeper layers of organizational knowledge to enhance negotiation practices will help to elevate the organization's negotiation practices and results at the table.
- **Mentoring takes over from training, at least beyond the foundational skills.** Peers and mentors become much more important as the move toward Adaptive Flexibility takes shape. Once a basic foundation of skills is present, the focus for ongoing skill building is through mentoring and peer engagement where new skills can be tailored to the local culture far more effectively.
- **Adaptations are not siloed.** The adaptations and learnings driven by Level 3 practices in one area are quickly shared to help elevate and inspire other creative negotiation approaches throughout the organization.
- **Hiring is more about capability and fit.** With a greater understanding of what knowledge, beliefs, and attitudes thrive in your organization's negotiation culture, hiring is much more about capability and fit than experience. The organization becomes much better at supporting and developing effective negotiators by starting with people predisposed to working within the organizational culture.
- **Barriers are identified quickly.** So much of what holds back talented individuals in negotiation are the organizational barriers, the friction that grinds good practice to a halt. Level 3 negotiation organizations encourage, support, and celebrate the identification of barriers and resistance points that make rapid change possible.
- **The difference between Ad Hockery and Adaptability is well understood.** To the untrained eye, an organization that has a variety of negotiation practices might look the same as an organization in Ad Hockery. However, there is a significant difference between organizations living in chaos and those which are adaptive and flexible based on good information and a strong foundation of competent practice.
- **Measurement drives improvement much like it supports repeatability.** While measurement is critical in ensuring consistent practice, it becomes equally central to identifying areas for adapting and improving those very practices. Using measurement this way supports a base of sound negotiation practice while identifying new approaches that raise these practices to new levels.

Everything described earlier starts with the implementation of clear practices in a repeatable and measurable way by establishing Level 2. Level 3: Adaptive Flexibility is the evolution born out of Level 2 success.

For the negotiation process, the framework and categories of the six key performance areas (KPAs) remain the same, with the same direct points of alignment between organizational KPAs and individual KPAs. The focus remains within the organization, on building flexible and responsive negotiation practices internally. It is in the area of Key Practices where important changes take place, changes that raise the bar and help the organization evolve to a higher level of performance at the bargaining table.

The NCM—Level 3 Adaptive Flexibility

As we saw in Chapter 4, there are three organizational KPAs, and these three areas are paired and aligned with three KPAs of individual competence. These areas remain the focus as the organization builds from Repeatable Competency to Adaptive Flexibility.

KPA #1: Strategy, Values, and Direction (SVD)

The purpose of the SVD KPA for Level 3 is to ensure the organization's values continue to serve as the foundation of the negotiation process while a new level of continuous improvement and learning takes hold. Once the organization has built a clear set of practices at Level 2, it can start to try new approaches, adapt to each different negotiation, and find new best practices to apply. All the while, these activities remain firmly connected to the overall SVD that the organization has set.

The goal of the SVD KPA at Level 3 is to support creativity and flexibility while preserving and maintaining the core values established in Level 2. As is the case in Level 2, the SVD KPA is directly aligned with the Individual Fit KPA for Level 3.

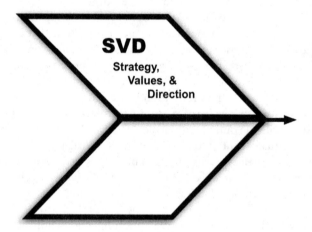

Figure 5.1 Strategy, Values, and Direction KPA—Level 3

While the SVD performance area remains the primary guiding force that governs all negotiation processes and procedures, it is now supported with in-depth measurements that enable negotiators to change and vary how they plan and execute each negotiation. Within the strategy and values of the organization, negotiators can start to emphasize the art of negotiation, while staying firmly grounded in a framework that has been engineered for success. Level 2 engineers the foundational negotiation activities; Level 3 opens up the canvas for full creativity.

The SVD practice area, for Level 3, is critical in ensuring that variation in the established negotiation process is purposeful and deliberate rather than a result of individual preferences or unconscious biases as seen in Ad Hockery. Staying anchored in SVD maintains a consistent framework and also allows negotiators to introduce changes and adaptations that respond to the unique circumstances in each negotiation.

So, how does the organization evolve from closely following the same process each time to tailoring each negotiation process as needed?

Key Capabilities and Key Practices SVD—Level 3

The Level 3 SVD capabilities that guide the negotiation process to adaptive flexibility include:

1. **An ability to uniquely apply core organizational and negotiation values to different functions within the organization.**
   While the overall values that provide direction for the organization are likely quite stable, the ability to apply them in unique and innovative ways becomes a hallmark of a Level 3 organization. The organization's values must not become a dusty poster hung on a wall that few pay attention to. These values must be applied directly to the challenges that negotiators face when making important decisions at the table and must be questioned and adapted where necessary.

   SVD Key Practice #1: Organizational values are questioned, adapted, and applied in unique ways to different functions within the organization.

   - How might different functions change and improve their negotiation approaches while remaining consistent and true to the organizational values?
   - Where does consistency stop adding value to the process and indicate a need for Adaptive Flexibility?
   - When and how do the lived experiences at the negotiating table cause the organization to refine or adjust its values?

   It is this constant process of reflection and evaluation that drives the adaptation, allowing the organization to find solutions and outcomes tailored to each situation.

2. **A robust ability to regularly review and improve specific negotiation processes and procedures.** Normalizing change and adaptation as part of the organizational strategy around negotiation allows for rapid growth and improvement. By continuously looking

for incremental improvement, change is accomplished with minimum resistance and maximum results.

SVD Key Practice #2: All negotiation processes and procedures are proactively reviewed, assessed, and improved, including approaches that create innovative new strategies.

- What strengths and weaknesses exist with the current negotiation processes and procedures?
- What opportunities, big or small, are presenting themselves?
- What do current negotiators find most useful and successful in the current organizational negotiation toolbox? What hasn't been successful?
- What needs have not been fully met?
- What external factors create new challenges for negotiations across the organization?

3. **An ability to strategically link negotiation ideas and adaptations across different areas of the organization.**
Adaptive flexibility isn't just allowing for variation across different negotiations, it also helps coordinate creative approaches across many functions in the organization, allowing it to disrupt the status quo and respond quickly to emerging challenges. This networked approach to negotiation strategy shares ideas and learnings rapidly while also responding to the unique needs and circumstances locally.

SVD Key Practice #3: Negotiation strategies are linked across different areas of the organization to broaden the strategic impact of negotiation.

- Where are the areas within the organization that negotiation provides the most critical strategic advantage?
- How can those areas partner with other parts of the organization to support learning and adaptation internally?
- How can an area make changes without having unintended consequences on other areas of the organization?
- Which stakeholders must be involved in reimagining a negotiation approach?

4. **Ability to learn from specific negotiation data and trends.** One of the reasons it's nearly impossible to go directly from Level 1: Ad Hockery to Level 3: Adaptive Flexibility is the missing data and knowledge that is built and established at Level 2: Repeatable Competency. Without the simple, repeatable activities established at Level 2, it is almost impossible to predict whether the strategies implemented at Level 3 will have positive and desired outcomes. In addition, without the metrics established at Level 2, negotiators lack the information to adapt successfully. Incorporating negotiation data into all facets of negotiation preparation and

evaluation is critical for Adaptive Flexibility, not just at the process level but also at the individual negotiation level. This increased knowledge base allows the organization to leverage more detailed Scorecard and KPI data to drive continuous improvement. Once KPIs are used to assess each negotiation, the next step is to link KPIs across the organization's negotiation activities to improve the process more broadly. This creates organization-wide learning and ensures best practices are shared, making negotiation a core cultural advantage.

SVD Key Practice #4A: Measurements and KPIs are used to track and measure variations and improvements for a range of processes that negotiators use.

- Where do existing measures highlight the need to evolve?
- Where are the data and evaluation gaps that need to be addressed with new tools or measurements?
- How effective are the organizational negotiation planning processes?
- How are individual negotiation successes measured?

SVD Key Practice #4B: Basic scorecard and other KPI data is compared across the organization and is reviewed for patterns and trends that lead to continuous improvement.

- What is the forum for gathering and comparing KPIs and other data across the organization?
- What learnings and best practices can be shared and operationalized based on the patterns and trends in the data?

5. **Ability to leverage internal expertise and mentors to drive innovation in negotiation planning, strategy, and evaluation.** One of the hidden organizational advantages around negotiation is being able to fully leverage peer input and learning across negotiation situations. Engaging with colleagues across negotiations serves not only to support individual negotiation success but also to spread adaptive best practices across different functional areas of the organization.

SVD Key Practice #5: The peer review process is well established and is a key step in driving negotiation planning, strategy, and evaluation.

- How can peers across the organization assist each other in preparing for key negotiations and adapting individual negotiation plans?
- How can peers across the organization help in understanding what did and didn't work?

Summary—Strategy, Values, and Direction KPA Level 3

At Level 3, the key goal of the SVD KPA is to keep everyone anchored around the organization's strategy, values, and direction while at the same time providing some breathing room for innovative adaptation. This flexibility in negotiation capabilities is driven by improving the organization's knowledge through core measurements and better information.

KPA #2: Individual Fit (IF)

The purpose of the Individual Fit KPA for Level 3 is to ensure that individuals are actively engaging in innovative negotiation practices in ways that support the organizational SVD. Ensuring that individual negotiators are empowered to be inventive while staying aligned with the larger organizational framework is critical.

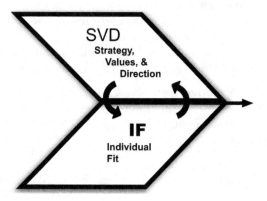

Figure 5.2 Individual Fit KPA—Level 3

Key Capabilities and Practices—IF

While the IF performance area remains closely aligned with the SVD practice area, the ability to leverage the bidirectional nature of shaping the SVD takes on greater importance. These Level 3 adaptive Individual Fit capabilities include:

1. **Ability for individuals to operationalize core organizational values in all of their negotiation practices.**
   As individuals begin to explore innovation and adaptation in the negotiation process, shared core values and their application take on greater importance.

   IF Key Practice #1A: Individuals adapt their own practices to implement the organization's values in all their negotiation practices.

   - What innovative individual practices that are consistent with the organization's values are developed?
   - What individual practices might have value for others in the organization, if shared?

IF Key Practice #1B: Individuals lead each negotiation in a way that guides all parties toward constructive negotiation approaches.

- How can individuals lead constructive processes in their negotiations when working with parties who may not be able to do so?
- How can individuals avoid negotiations sinking to the lowest common denominator within the negotiation process?

IF Key Practice #1C: Individuals are able to anticipate when negotiation partners are likely to become competitive and distributive, and can adapt their own practices to remain integrative wherever possible.

- How can individuals recognize distributive behavior in other parties early?
- What steps can be taken to shift this dynamic toward a more integrative approach?

2. **Ability for individuals to contribute to continuous improvement around all negotiation processes.**
   Each individual must make ongoing improvement and adaptation a critical part of their practice.

   IF Key Practice #2A: Individuals actively participate in refining and adapting roles and responsibilities to support negotiation best practices.

   - What roles and responsibilities are key in your organization's negotiation processes?
   - How do they vary from functional area to functional area?
   - How can key negotiation responsibilities best be integrated into existing roles?

   IF Key Practice #2B: Individuals proactively reflect on and evaluate past negotiations to support organizational improvement.

   - How can reflection and assessment be normalized and operationalized?
   - How can individuals be supported to proactively find ways for the organization to improve?

   IF Key Practice #2C: Individuals share best practices and adaptations to the planning, preparation, and execution processes with negotiation colleagues across the organization.

   - How can individual innovation be shared and broadened around the negotiation function?
   - What tools can be put in place to operationalize this sharing?

3. **Ability for individuals to ensure that measurements serve as key drivers in negotiation processes.**
   Measurement in Level 3 takes on greater value in improving practices.

   IF Key Practice #3: Negotiators regularly adapt measurements and KPIs to improve their value as drivers of the negotiation process.

Summary—Individual Fit KPA

At Level 3, the IF performance area is paramount in maintaining individual commitment to the organizational framework. The IF area, when aligned with SVD, establishes a framework to allow for more individualized approaches, provided they remain within the overall SVD of the organization.

KPA #3: Human Capital and Organizational Investment (HCOI)

The purpose of the HCOI KPA for Level 3 is to take the organization past Level 2 by ensuring that investment is made to hire individuals with a continuous improvement mindset and by investing the resources needed for fostering and supporting an adaptive negotiation culture. HCOI remains linked to the individual KS KPA and is the organizational engine to identify individuals who will thrive in an adaptive environment and support them in doing so.

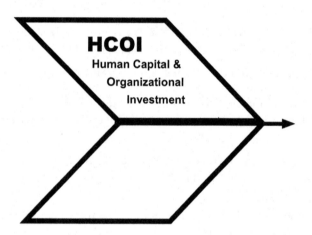

Figure 5.3 Human Capital and Organizational Investment KPA—Level 3

Key Capabilities and Practices—HCOI

These Level 3 adaptive HCOI KPA capabilities include:

1. **An ability to consistently hire and retain individuals capable of contributing to a cutting-edge negotiation culture targeted at continuous improvement and adaptation.**

   HCOI Key Practice #1: Hiring criteria are refined to identify individuals committed to integrative negotiation approaches as a baseline, as well as a capacity to adapt and flex their negotiation practices toward continuous improvement.

- What specific attributes are evaluated and prioritized during the hiring process to ensure an entrepreneurial approach to building better negotiation skills and abilities?
- What processes are in place to provide feedback to hiring managers about what to look for during the hiring process?

2. **An ability to support and invest in successful negotiation practice and performance activities.**

   HCOI Key Practice #2A: Negotiation preparation, practice activities, outcomes, and self-reflection are deeply embedded in performance and evaluation processes.

   - What performance and evaluation processes are in place to ensure that direct feedback and guidance are given to negotiators on a regular basis?

   HCOI Key Practice #2B: The organization demonstrates investment in recognition and promotion of innovative negotiation practices.

   - How clearly are desired negotiation behaviors and successes celebrated and rewarded as a means of supporting the organizational culture around negotiation practices?

3. **An ability to invest in key organizational supports that deliver necessary knowledge and tools to support the negotiation function.**

   HCOI Key Practice #3A: Significant organizational investment is allocated to integrating and embedding best practices in the negotiation process, such as research, technology and databases, and administrative support.

   - What infrastructure is in place to capture and share negotiation best practices?
   - What technology is needed to ensure that all individuals have easy access to core tools and information around negotiation within the organization?

   HCOI Key Practice #3B: Training resources are continually updated, improved, and adapted to the specific goals and values of the organization.

   - How are training resources made relevant to your organization on an ongoing basis? How is skill and knowledge training tailored to the issues and concerns of negotiators?
   - How much input is solicited from individual negotiators into the training and learning goals of the organization?

HCOI Key Practice #3C: Activity-based metrics are continuously reviewed and refined as a critical part of the organization's negotiation learning and development resources.

• What metrics are captured and used as learning and development tools?

4. **An ability to offer education that develops knowledge and skills specific to all functional areas in the organization.**

HCOI Key Practice #4A: Individual development plans ensure that negotiators become more than familiar with the strategic and operational needs of the areas they negotiate for.

• Are individual development plans delivering the local knowledge needed at the bargaining table?

Summary—Human Capital and Organizational Investment KPA

At Level 3, HCOI must help elevate the infrastructure needed to develop an adaptive and flexible approach to negotiations, without losing the foundation of repeatability built in Level 2.

KPA #4: Knowledge and Skills

The purpose of the KS KPA for Level 3 is to help individuals become actively engaged in their own continuous learning that aligns with the organizational continuous improvement cycle. Aligning the KS KPA with the HCOI KPA ensures that negotiators working toward new and flexible approaches to negotiation are supported and resourced.

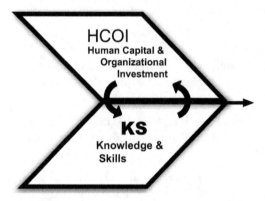

Figure 5.4 Knowledge and Skills KPA—Level 3

Key Capabilities and Practices—KS

At Level 3, individuals must follow the organization's lead in becoming adaptive and innovative in their practices. The following key practices are necessary at Level 3:

1. **An ability for individuals to reflect on and give feedback to the organization to ensure continuous improvement and flexibility.**

   KS Key Practice #1A: Negotiators assume significant responsibility for improving and adapting the negotiation process itself.

   - What contributions do individual negotiators make to sharing ideas and needs for improvement?
   - How can individual innovation be replicated?

   KS Key Practice #1B: Individual negotiators regularly engage in post-negotiation audits as a critical part of the continuous improvement cycle.

   - Is there a clear process for conducting post-negotiation audits or assessments?
   - How is information from those audits captured and shared?
   - Are the audits understood as critical for driving key learnings for the organization?

   KS Key Practice #1C: Individuals seek innovative and new approaches in their individual negotiation practices, and freely share these innovations with their colleagues and the organization.

   - Do individual negotiators share their successes and failures as they test changes and adaptations to the established negotiation processes?

2. **Individuals demonstrate the advanced negotiation skills necessary for adapting to the specific challenges in each negotiation situation.**

   KS Key Practice #2A: Individuals assess the skill level of their negotiation counterparts and have an ability to guide negotiations successfully with weak or inexperienced negotiators on the other side.

   - How effectively does the training curriculum prepare negotiators to work with weaker or less experienced negotiators on the other side?
   - Is there a repository for documenting previous experiences with repeat negotiation partners?

KS Key Practice #2B: Individuals can demonstrate the following advanced skills, at a minimum:

- Applies common negotiation styles and frames regularly:

    o Directs and sustains negotiations toward integrative processes/value creating situations
    o Names distributive negotiation/value claiming situations and leads both parties toward integrative approaches wherever appropriate

- Addresses negotiation power/strength issues during negotiations to prevent adversarial strategies from developing
- Consistently engages all parties through their interests as a primary goal in negotiation
- Consistently tests and engages other parties around their targets, resistance points, motives, and feelings of confidence
- Consistently applies advanced engagement skills such as strategic questioning and listening,[1] relationship building, reciprocity,[2] loss aversion,[3] and rigorous value creation during the negotiation process
- Directly applies their own side's BATNAs[4] and WATNAs to their negotiation strategy

    o Leverages the other side's BATNAs and WATNAs toward outcomes that benefit both parties

- Consistently seeks to strengthen long-term relationships throughout the negotiation process independent of outcome

3. **Ability to effectively connect with peers and mentors across the organization to build negotiation knowledge and skill sharing.**

    KS Key Practice #3—Peer groups and mentors within the organization meet regularly around negotiation to share knowledge and innovations key to negotiation success.

    - Do individuals commit to regularly meeting and sharing knowledge and ideas around negotiation?
    - Is this knowledge captured and shared in a readily accessible way?

Summary—Knowledge and Skills KPA

At Level 3, individuals must take the lead in advancing a creative approach to all negotiations, with clear support from the HCOI performance area. Once the foundation has been created in Level 2 and a clear and systemic approach is in place, new approaches and new strategies at the table can be brought into play.

KPA #5: Organizational Incentives (OI)

The purpose of the OI KPA for Level 3 is to ensure that the incentives for negotiation staff support both the foundational Level 2: Repeatable Competency and the Level 3: Adaptive Flexibility capabilities. Special attention is paid to unintended impacts around incentives.

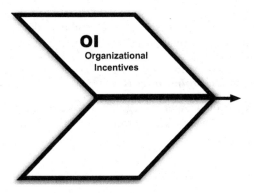

Figure 5.5 Organizational Incentives KPA—Level 3

Key Capabilities and Practices—OI

At Level 3, incentives must be scrutinized even more carefully to ensure they are guiding negotiators toward creative and innovative practices. The following key practices are necessary at Level 3:

1. **Ability to ensure that incentives, both monetary and nonmonetary, support adaptive and flexible negotiation processes and practices.**

   OI Key Practice #1A: Incentive programs are assessed, designed, and implemented to ensure individual negotiators support a culture of continuous improvement and adaptation within the organization.

   - Are monetary incentive programs regularly audited to ensure alignment with innovative negotiation practices and risk-taking?
   - Are nonmonetary incentives reviewed to avoid unintended consequences?

   OI Key Practice #1B: Individual interests of negotiation staff are gathered and assessed regularly.

   - Are there frequent opportunities for individuals to share their own interests around negotiations to help the organization identify opportunities for adaptation?

2. **Ability to define clear promotional opportunities and career paths that incorporate negotiation competencies and successes.**

    OI Key Practice #2: Career paths are developed to maximize retention of negotiation staff, and promotion practices support individuals who demonstrate leadership around adaptive and creative negotiation competencies.

    -   Are there well-developed and well-publicized career paths related to negotiation competencies?

Summary—Organizational Incentives KPA

At Level 3, OI takes on a larger role, going beyond eliminating disincentives and actively creating incentives that promote creative, flexible, and adaptable negotiation practices.

KPA #6: Individual Interests (II)

The purpose of the II KPA is to understand the individual interests of negotiation staff and ensure these interests are aligned with the organization as it moves toward Level 3 Adaptive Flexibility. The II KPA links directly to the OI KPA.

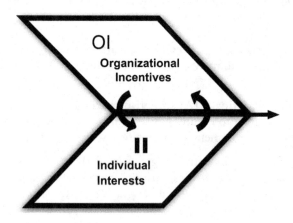

Figure 5.6 Individual Interests KPA—Level 3

1. **Ability to communicate II and seek alignment with OI as the organization focuses on Adaptive Flexibility in the negotiation process.**

II Key Practice #1A: Individuals follow up to ensure their interests are incorporated into OI.

- Do individuals actively share their core interests to ensure they are incorporated into the organizational incentive structures?

II Key Practice #1B: Individuals engage actively in cross-functional relationships across the organization in support of overall negotiation successes.

- Do individuals actively connect with peers across different functions to support alignment and best practices in negotiation?

2. **Ability for individuals to identify misalignment between OI and II.**

   II Key Practice #2: Individuals raise misalignment issues and mixed-motive problems through agreed processes quickly.

- Are individuals supported and celebrated for raising alignment issues around OI and II?
- Do individuals articulate mixed motive challenges quickly to help maintain alignment?

Summary—Individual Interests KPA

At Level 3, individuals are expected to communicate their important interests and actively work with the organization to maintain alignment between their interests and OI.

Summary—The NCM at Level 3

In summary, to achieve Level 3, a new set of key practices must be introduced that build on the foundation of Level 2, yet go further into flexible and innovative new approaches. Individual negotiators must adapt and respond to the unique needs of each individual negotiation while avoiding the pitfall of slipping back into Ad Hockery.

Key Practices Condensed—Level 3: Adaptive Flexibility

A summary of the Level 3 key practices includes the following:

Strategy, Values, and Direction:

SVD Key Practice #1: Organizational values are questioned, adapted, and applied in unique ways to different functions within the organization.

SVD Key Practice #2: All negotiation processes and procedures are proactively reviewed, assessed, and improved, including approaches that create innovative new strategies.

SVD Key Practice #3: Negotiation strategies are linked across different areas of the organization to broaden the strategic impact of negotiation.

SVD Key Practice #4A: Measurements and KPIs are used to track and measure variations and improvements for a range of processes that negotiators use.

SVD Key Practice #4B: Basic Scorecard and other KPI data are compared across the organization and are reviewed for patterns and trends that lead to continuous improvement.

SVD Key Practice #5: The peer review process is well established and is a key step in driving negotiation planning, strategy, and evaluation.

Individual Fit:

IF Key Practice #1A: Individuals adapt their own practices to implement the organization's values in all their negotiation practices.

IF Key Practice #1B: Individuals lead each negotiation in a way that guides all parties toward constructive negotiation approaches.

IF Key Practice #1C: Individuals are able to anticipate when negotiation partners are likely to become competitive and distributive and can adapt their own practices to remain integrative wherever possible.

IF Key Practice #2A: Individuals actively participate in refining and adapting roles and responsibilities to support negotiation best practices.

IF Key Practice #2B: Individuals proactively reflect on and evaluate past negotiations to support organizational improvement.

IF Key Practice #2C: Individuals share best practices and adaptations to the planning, preparation, and execution processes with negotiation colleagues across the organization.

IF Key Practice #3: Negotiators regularly adapt measurements and KPIs to improve their value as drivers of the negotiation process.

Human Capital and Organizational Investment:

HCOI Key Practice #1: Hiring criteria are refined to identify individuals committed to integrative negotiation approaches as a baseline, as well as a capacity to adapt and flex their negotiation practices toward continuous improvement.

HCOI Key Practice #2A: Negotiation preparation, practice activities, outcomes, and self-reflection are deeply embedded in performance and evaluation processes.

HCOI Key Practice #2B: The organization demonstrates investment in recognition and promotion of innovative negotiation practices.

HCOI Key Practice #3A: Significant organizational investment is allocated to integrating and embedding best practices in the negotiation process, such as research, technology and databases, and administrative support.

HCOI Key Practice #3B: Training resources are continually updated, improved, and adapted to the specific goals and values of the organization.

HCOI Key Practice #3C: Activity-based metrics are continuously reviewed and refined as a critical part of the organization's negotiation learning and development resources.

HCOI Key Practice #4A: Individual development plans ensure that negotiators become more than familiar with the strategic and operational needs of the areas they negotiate for.

Knowledge and Skills:

KS Key Practice #1A: Negotiators assume significant responsibility for improving and adapting the negotiation process itself.

KS Key Practice #1B: Individual negotiators regularly engage in post-negotiation audits as a critical part of the continuous improvement cycle.

KS Key Practice #1C: Individuals seek innovative and new approaches in their individual negotiation practices, and freely share these innovations with their colleagues and the organization.

KS Key Practice #2A: Individuals assess the skill level of their negotiation counterparts and have an ability to guide negotiations successfully with weak or inexperienced negotiators on the other side.

KS Key Practice #2B: Individuals are able to demonstrate the following advanced skills at a minimum:

- Applies common negotiation styles and frames regularly
    - o Directs and sustains negotiations toward integrative processes/value-creating situations
    - o Names distributive negotiation/value claiming situations and leads both parties toward integrative approaches wherever appropriate

- Addresses negotiation power/strength issues during negotiations to prevent adversarial strategies from developing
- Consistently engages all parties through their interests as a primary goal in negotiation
- Consistently tests and engages other parties around their targets, resistance points, motives, and feelings of confidence
- Consistently applies advanced engagement skills such as strategic questioning and listening,[5] relationship building, reciprocity,[6] loss aversion,[7] and rigorous value creation during the negotiation process
- Directly applies their own side's BATNAs[8] and WATNAs to their negotiation strategy
  o Leverages the other side's BATNAs and WATNAs toward outcomes that benefit both parties

- Consistently seeks to strengthen long-term relationships throughout the negotiation process independent of outcome

KS Key Practice #3—Peer groups and mentors within the organization meet regularly around negotiation to share knowledge and innovations key to negotiation success.

Organizational Incentives:

OI Key Practice #1A: Incentive programs are assessed, designed, and implemented to ensure individual negotiators support a culture of continuous improvement and adaptation within the organization.

OI Key Practice #1B: Individual interests of negotiation staff are gathered and assessed regularly.

OI Key Practice #2: Career paths are developed to maximize retention of negotiation staff, and promotion practices support individuals who demonstrate leadership around organizational negotiation competencies.

Individual Interests:

II Key Practice #1A: Individuals follow up to ensure their interests are incorporated into organizational incentives.

II Key Practice #1B: Individuals engage actively in cross-functional relationships across the organization in support of overall negotiation successes.

II Key Practice #2: Individuals raise misalignment issues and mixed-motive problems through agreed processes quickly.

Notes

1 Furlong, G., & Harrison, J. (2018). *Brain fishing: A practice guide to questioning skills.* Friesen Press.
2 Furlong, G. T. (2020). *The conflict resolution toolbox.* John Wiley & Sons, Chapter 8 The Law of Reciprocity.
3 Furlong, G. T. (2020). *The conflict resolution toolbox,* John Wiley & Sons, Chapter 9 The Loss Aversion Bias.
4 Fisher, R., & Ury, W. (1981). *Getting to yes: Negotiating agreement without giving in.* Houghton Mifflin Co.
5 Furlong, G., & Harrison, J. (2018). *Brain fishing: A practice guide to questioning skills.* Friesen Press.
6 Furlong, G. T. (2020). *The conflict resolution toolbox,* John Wiley & Sons, Chapter 8 The Law of Reciprocity
7 Furlong, G. T. (2020). *The conflict resolution toolbox,* John Wiley & Sons, Chapter 9 The Loss Aversion Bias
8 Fisher, R., & Ury, W. (1981). *Getting to yes: Negotiating agreement without giving in.* Houghton Mifflin Co.

6   Level 4 NCM—Optimized Performance

Introduction

We started by moving out of Ad Hockery and into repeatable processes, then moved from this basic repeatability into Adaptive Flexibility, where innovation and artistry can grow from a foundation of repeatable consistency. We are now looking at the final step of the NCM, Optimized Performance.

The first three states of the NCM, Level 1: Ad Hockery; Level 2: Repeatable Competency; and Level 3: Adaptive Flexibility, tend to be focused on the processes and approaches within the organization—what the organization itself can do internally to improve its negotiation processes. In Ad Hockery, negotiators are highly reactive to whatever conditions or bumps in the road come their way, with little support or strategic direction from the organization. In Level 2, the organization and the negotiators build a consistent framework and process to follow to achieve their specific negotiation mandates. In Level 3, that framework begins to go beyond consistent and repeatable negotiation processes by starting to apply creative and adaptive approaches that deliver even better outcomes. In addition, these adaptive approaches are integrated across the organization to embed a culture of negotiation expertise. In all three levels, the focus is within the organization, on the structures, processes, and choices the people and the organization can control and influence directly.

We now come to Level 4 of the NCM. To truly optimize the value that effective negotiation can provide, there are limits to what one party, any one party, can achieve unilaterally by focusing their strategy and actions internally. At some point, the very structure of the negotiation itself must be challenged and changed. The most effective way to do this is by both parties at the table coming together to jointly design the goals, structure, and context of the negotiation process right from the beginning. It may even require that the parties disrupt or challenge established practices and beliefs at a deep level to unlock or create value that simply wasn't seen before. And this requires negotiators to focus externally and collaboratively, to work together to define or redefine basic assumptions to reach Level 4.

DOI:10.4324/9781003243854-7

In this chapter, we will explore the final level from the NCM—Optimized Performance—and lay out a vision for fundamental change and value creation through the negotiation process itself.

Status Quo and Fundamental Change

In almost every negotiation, the parameters of what is being negotiated are set and accepted long before the negotiation starts. Often, today's negotiation is simply an extension or repeat of how we negotiated the last time around. In a procurement negotiation, the company typically sends out a Request for Proposal (RFP) detailing the scope and nature of the product or service needed, the duration of the contract, the qualifications required, and so on. Every significant aspect of the arrangement is predetermined, and for the sake of simplicity, this year's RFP is based on the previous one, which was based on the one before that, with minor updates and modifications at best. Should a service provider send in a proposal with ideas for a completely different approach, that is, suggest a different product to meet the customer's needs or a completely different way to provide value, in many cases they will simply be considered "non-compliant" with the RFP process and disqualified. In other words, if I ask to purchase a car from you and you offer to lease it to me instead, I may not even consider the request.

Unfortunately, while improving the repeatability and flexibility of an organization's negotiation skills internally are critical steps, a great deal of potential value in any negotiation can be missed—for both parties. It is only by developing the ability to jointly optimize value, to jointly challenge the accepted norms, by challenging "this is the way we do things" at a deeper level—and doing so together—that deeper benefits can be realized. In other words, the parties need to know how to negotiate the very process of the negotiation itself. And that can only be done collaboratively, where parties design the negotiation framework together as a way to unlock ideas that are simply not available when negotiating "against" another party. When parties negotiate to increase and maximize value first, before negotiating how they will share that value, there is simply more value available for both parties to work with. When the water level itself rises, all boats rise as well.

Optimized Performance requires us to look at the negotiation process from a very different perspective. Negotiation, as we saw, is characterized in many ways, such as a dance, a sports competition, or even a marriage. What is common to all these metaphors is the idea that it takes two (or more) to tango, as the saying goes. The outcome, in other words, depends less on what I choose to do individually and more on what we choose to do together. The best dancer in the world will look foolish if their partner is unskilled, and the best negotiator in the world can appear to have failed if the other party simply won't come to the table or agree to even a basic agenda.

An optimized approach, on the other hand, brings together the expertise and perspectives of both parties. It recognizes that complex challenges require the collective creativity of all parties, that better solutions may be available only through full collaboration. It allows each party to benefit from the knowledge, ideas, and perspectives of the other party or parties both before and during a negotiation, information typically not available to each other in most negotiation processes.

A Partnered Approach to Negotiation

To achieve this optimized performance, an entirely different approach to negotiation, from start to finish, must be found. This approach, often called a "partnered approach," starts well before the parties sit at a bargaining table. It starts with a pre-bargaining discussion or dialogue that focuses on the negotiation process itself, on understanding the goals of each party, on what needs to be negotiated, and what each party expects when the negotiation starts. It uncovers the core assumptions each party is making, it asks the question "Why?," challenging each parties' thinking and reasons. All of this is done with the goal of accessing each parties' knowledge, skill, and information to make sure all the value that can be achieved is explored—jointly.

A fundamental reason human beings negotiate and work together is because of complexity. The reason a property owner hires an architect is because the owner has one important piece of the puzzle—land—and the architect has another piece—ideas for a building that meets the owner's needs. When the contractor is hired, the contractor has another important piece of the puzzle—the ability to construct the building. Another party, the supplier, adds another critical piece—sourcing the supplies the contractor needs. Each needs the other's knowledge and skills to construct a building that meets the needs of the owner and the tenants. Each has information the other simply doesn't have, and unless we share that information, in some way, nothing useful can be achieved.

The parties have a choice as to how this process unfolds, however. They can communicate the least amount of information possible to maintain what they see as their "advantage" in the negotiation. The supplier gives the contractor a fixed price for building materials, nothing more, which the contractor doesn't share with the owner; the contractor also gives the owner a fixed price, nothing more. None of the parties may know anything other than the price. For the owner to learn anything, they will be forced to get three, maybe four competing bids—also just fixed prices—and try to figure out why one price is dramatically higher or lower than some of the others. Is it quality? Is it different materials or different construction methods? Is one contractor busy, the other needing work? When knowledge is seen as power in negotiations, as it often is, little information is shared: The negotiation process becomes more of a guessing game, a process of pressure, demands, and brinkmanship, one that is likely to be inefficient and expensive for at least one, perhaps all, parties.

Another alternative is for parties to meet before any negotiations take place and share information instead. The supplier can break down the costs—some materials are expensive, others relatively cheap. The contractor can use this information to guide the owner toward some design changes that improve the final product and reduce the cost. The owner can share the important uses for the building, allowing the architect to make suggestions that improve the performance and value of the property, adding value for the owner at no additional cost to the architect or contractor. By the time the parties finalize the price, schedule, and materials, all parties have already gained value. Each party has contributed to increasing the overall pool of value, making it likely that all parties will do better than they could have when knowledge was hoarded as leverage.

This partnered approach, however, is counterintuitive, as it requires parties to see negotiation not as something to win or do better than the other party but as an exercise in collaboration and value creation, one that can only be done working together, not individually.

At a minimum, this shift toward Optimized Performance through a partnered negotiation approach must consider the following ideas:

- **Negotiation is not an event; it is an ongoing process of value creation.** Pre-bargaining dialogue between the parties must become a necessary step where the parties look at the parameters of the negotiation, challenge the scope, understand value from all parties' point of view, and jointly look at how the negotiation process can serve everyone most effectively.
- **The definition of success in the negotiation must include sustainability for both parties.** At Levels 1, 2, and 3, success is typically defined as "my party getting what we need." At Level 4, success must include "both parties getting more than what they need." When success is defined this way, it unlocks value at a deeper layer.
- **Interests must be aligned.** All parties need to identify their interests, then focus on their common interests more than focusing on their competing interests.
- **Industry norms and standards are challenged.** The typical approach to negotiation, often embedded as industry standards or simply the "normal" way this is done, needs to be questioned. These norms, either conscious or unconscious, often limit the creativity and flexibility needed to find better solutions.

- **Data and information:** The adage Knowledge is Power must be revised to read Knowledge is Power—But Only When Everyone Has It. When knowledge is guarded, it is seen as a useful way to leverage the other side—a short-term strategy at best. When knowledge is seen as powerful because everyone has it, when everyone uses it to find better solutions and make better decisions, it becomes a sustainable source of advantage for all parties involved. Joint data collection and pre-negotiation information exchanges all contribute to a partnered approach.
- **Supporting all parties at the table:** A partnered approach recognizes that if one party has little experience or poor negotiation skills, this will negatively impact all parties. A partnered approach helps everyone improve their preparation, information, and ability to create value, which again increases value for all parties.
- **Measurement:** Key performance measures from the negotiation itself can also be shared to establish the ongoing value of a partnered approach, making it a long-term strategy for the parties involved.

Everything described earlier starts with parties working together to design the negotiation itself, looking to jointly create value in the process as a first step. Only then will the full value available to the parties be realized. It should be noted, one more time, that not all negotiations need to be conducted at Level 4. In some situations, practicing and reaching Level 2 or 3 may strike the right balance for all parties to a negotiation. In other situations, however, only a partnered, Optimized Performance approach will create a long-term competitive advantage for both parties.

The NCM—Level 4 Optimized Performance

As we saw in Chapter 3, there are three key performance areas (KPAs) at the organizational level, and these three areas are paired and aligned with three KPAs of individual competence. That doesn't change at Level 4. We'll look at each KPA, linking each organizational competence with its directly aligned individual competency.

By the time an organization is focusing on Level 4, it means that it has created and begun to practice some or all of Level 2 and Level 3. With Level 2 and Level 3 in play, Level 4 can focus directly on the key practices (KPs) needed to achieve the most value for both parties in any negotiation.

KPA #1: Strategy, Values, and Direction (SVD)

The purpose of the SVD KPA for Level 4 is to introduce and embed the idea that deep engagement and collaboration with negotiation partners is a core value and strategy of the organization. The SVD key performance area is directly aligned with the Individual Fit KPA.

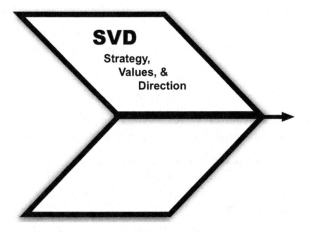

Figure 6.1 Strategy, Values, and Direction KPA—Level 4

Key Capabilities and Practices—SVD

For SVD at Level 4, the following capabilities must be identified as necessary for elevating the negotiation function, followed by implementation of key practices that deliver on those capabilities.

1. **Ability to introduce, promote, and reinforce a partnered approach to important negotiations.**
   For Level 4, the critical organizational value that needs to be supported and promoted is approaching important negotiations as a partnership exercise rather than a friendly (or other!) process of each party getting the most they can. The focus must move away from specific targets and outcomes and toward an exploration of value. Specific monetary targets limit the playing field to a narrow range of options. Value, however, can take many forms, often surprising to both parties, and can only be discovered when the parties are actively looking to create and build value rather than achieve narrow goals.

   SVD Key Practice #1A: A partnered approach to negotiations is embedded and communicated internally as part of the organization's values and strategies.

   • The organization must make this approach a part of its mission, vision, and values.

   SVD Key Practice #1B: Core organizational and negotiation values are regularly shared across the industry and with negotiation partners to advance effective negotiation approaches beyond the organization.

- By openly sharing a commitment to a partnered negotiation approach, more opportunities to explore value are created.

2. **Ability to develop and implement procedures, practices, roles, and responsibilities to introduce and implement a partnered negotiation approach.**
    The internal negotiation procedures and practices must support and direct negotiations toward a partnered approach.

    SVD Key Practice #2A: Negotiation strategies are expanded to include a collaborative, partnered approach with key organizations.

    - Each negotiation should include a mandatory assessment of whether a partnered approach should be employed—and if not, why not. While not all negotiations need or should be Level 4, it should be assessed for every negotiation.

    SVD Key Practice #2B: Specific negotiation processes and procedures have been developed to implement an interorganizational joint negotiation strategy.

    - The organization must develop the skills and processes to initiate and run a partnered negotiation process, where appropriate.

3. **Ability to integrate data, measurement, and KPIs directly related to partnered negotiations.**
    SVD Key Practice #3A: Critical data and information influencing the negotiation are routinely shared with negotiation partners whenever possible.
    SVD Key Practice #3B: Scorecard and KPI data is measured and tested against data from partnered organizations and industry.

    - Outcomes and results from partnered negotiations are compared to broader outcomes in the sector.

Summary—Strategy, Values, and Direction

A key goal of this SVD performance area is to introduce high-level expectations and overall strategy for a partnered approach into the negotiation function. Only when this optimized approach to creating value is endorsed at the strategy and values level will the organization see these tools used to everyone's benefit.

KPA #2: Individual Fit (IF)

The purpose of the IF KPA for Level 4 is to ensure that all individuals working in the negotiation space in the organization are fully aligned with engaging in a partnered approach to negotiation wherever possible. The tendency for individuals to fall back on competitive approaches to negotiation is strong, often resulting in negotiations that start collaboratively but slowly devolve into distributive contests to claim value. Level 4 IF ensures that the partnered negotiation approach is a strong focus for all individuals leading negotiations. The IF KPA is directly aligned with the organizational SVD KPA.

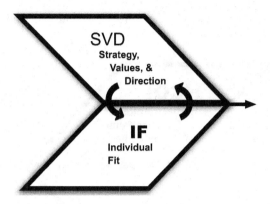

Figure 6.2 Individual Fit KPA—Level 4

Key Capabilities and Practices—IF

1. **Ability to advocate for a partnered approach to negotiation wherever appropriate.**

    IF Key Practice #1A: Individuals take a leadership role within their organization and industry to help other organizations and individuals explore the value of a partnered negotiation approach.

    IF Key Practice #1B: Individuals share best practices and adaptations to the partnered approach with negotiation colleagues across their industry.

2. **Ability to adapt and improve key measurements and data gathering directly related to a partnered approach.**

    IF Key Practice #2A: Negotiators include data gathering and data sharing into negotiation planning processes wherever possible.

    IF Key Practice #2B: Negotiators develop key measurements and KPIs to support industry best practices and share with key negotiation partners.

Summary—Individual Fit

When the SVD of an organization moves to Level 4, there must be a fit and alignment with all individuals in the negotiation function to support and implement Level 4, both at the table and more broadly within industry as well.

KPA #3: Human Capital and Organizational Investment (HCOI)

The purpose of the HCOI KPA for Level 4 is to ensure the organization has adapted its policies, procedures, and practices to align with a partnered negotiation strategy. In addition, it ensures the organization has invested in hiring, training, and supporting a partnered negotiation function across the organization. HCOI is directly linked to the individual Knowledge and Skills KPA.

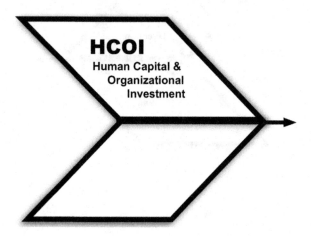

Figure 6.3 Human Capital and Organizational Investment KPA—Level 4

So what, specifically, should an organization be focused on and investing in when implementing a partnered negotiation strategy? The following competencies and practices will guide the organization toward strengthening and supporting its human capital in this aspect of the negotiation function.

Key Capabilities and Practices—HCOI

Since it's human nature to see the world from a self-centered perspective, organizations that want to explore joint value creation through the negotiation process must invest time and resources in supporting collaborative skills internally, engaging with negotiation partners externally, as well as exporting these approaches to industry.

For HCOI, the following capabilities are identified as necessary for a partnered approach, followed by implementation of key practices that deliver on those capabilities.

1. **Ability to identify and hire negotiation staff who are fully aligned with a partnered negotiation mindset.**

HCOI Key Practice #1: Hiring criteria contains a strong component of collaborative and partnered negotiation skills, experience, and values.

2. **Ability to invest in and support the promotion of value creation and collaborative negotiations beyond the organization.**

HCOI Key Practice #2A: Significant organizational investment is allocated to sharing and supporting best practices in the negotiation process with key negotiation partners and across the industry.

HCOI Key Practice #2B: Opportunities for shared training focused on a partnered approach with key negotiation partners are sought and supported.

3. **Ability to design and deliver targeted measurements that assess the value of partnered negotiation practices.**

HCOI Key Practice #3: Process-oriented success measures are developed internally and shared with key negotiation partners.

Summary—Human Capital and Organizational Investment

In addition to the key practices at Level 3, these additional practices will help the organization take the next step and engage negotiation partners fully in the value creation process.

KPA #4: Knowledge and Skills (KS)

The purpose of the KS KPA for Level 4 is to ensure that all individuals with negotiation responsibilities have the knowledge and skills to advocate for and deliver partnered negotiation processes with negotiation partners and industry. KS is directly aligned with the HCOI KPA.

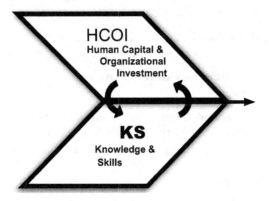

Figure 6.4 Knowledge and Skills KPA—Level 4

Key Capabilities and Practices

The following are the key capabilities and key practices (KPs) for individuals who are tasked with delivering a partnered negotiation approach.

1. **Ability to lead and deliver a partnered negotiation approach.**

    KS Key Practice #1: Individuals are able to demonstrate the following optimized skills at a minimum:

    -   Focus on pre-negotiation discussions with other parties well before any formal negotiations begin
    -   Manage and share meaningful data and information with other parties
    -   Understand and apply an integrative and collaborative approach that seeks mutual gains in negotiated solutions
    -   Actively defines and applies procedural trust[1] principles in all negotiations
    -   Seeks alignment of goals and common interests with negotiation partners as a primary strategy
    -   Analyzes negotiations to include the interests and impacts beyond the parties at the table
    -   Identifies all barriers and challenges as a joint set of problems to solve
    -   Sees conflict as a starting point, not an end point, of the negotiation
    -   Builds clear issue resolution processes for resolving problems in between formal negotiations

2. **Ability to work with industry and negotiation partners in an optimized partnership approach.**

    KS Key Practice #2A: Individuals share advanced tools and expert information around negotiation practices with key negotiation partners to improve negotiation capabilities.

    KS Key Practice #2B: Industry peer groups meet regularly around negotiation to share knowledge and innovations key to negotiation success.

    KS Key Practice #2C: Regulatory or governance barriers to partnered negotiation processes are identified and targeted for change.

3. **Ability to continuously develop and enhance a partnered negotiation approach.**

    KS Key Practice #3: Post-negotiation audits are conducted that include all negotiation partners, and information on improving negotiation practices are shared to support continuous improvement.

Summary—Knowledge and Skills

The KS performance area at Level 4 requires that individual negotiators both buy-in to a partnered negotiation approach and build and maintain the skill and ability to work collaboratively with parties in each negotiation.

KPA #5: Organizational Incentives (OI)

The purpose of the OI KPA for Level 4 is to ensure the organization has created incentives that promote a partnered approach to negotiation. Incentives need to be aligned in a way that guides negotiators toward considering and implementing partnered negotiations wherever it will create value. OI is directly linked to the Individual Interests KPA.

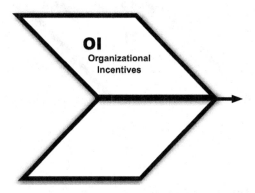

Figure 6.5 Organizational Incentives KPA—Level 4

Key Capabilities and Practices—OI

For OI, the following capabilities and key practices for a partnered negotiation approach need to be considered.

1. **Ability to strategically design both monetary and nonmonetary incentives to encourage a partnered negotiation approach wherever appropriate.**

   OI Key Practice #1: Incentive programs are assessed and designed in a way that motivates negotiators to explore and implement a partnered approach to negotiation with key negotiation partners.

Summary—Organizational Incentives

The OI KPA at Level 4 is focused, quite simply, on creating incentives to bargain collaboratively from the beginning. Level 4 is where the true value of a mutual gains approach can be realized.

KPA #6: Individual Interests (II)

The purpose of the II KPA is to ensure that the individual interests of negotiation staff continue to be aligned with the interests of the organization when implementing partnered negotiation approaches. II is directly linked to the OI KPA.

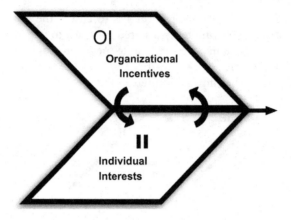

Figure 6.6 Individual Interests KPA—Level 4

Key Capabilities and Practices—II

1. **Ability to align individual interests with a partnered negotiation approach and to identify misalignments quickly and clearly.**
    In the spirit of a partnered approach to the negotiation process, a partnered approach is also required between negotiation staff and the organization. Individuals need to participate in ensuring alignment of their interests with the organization's interests and be able to communicate directly when any misalignment takes place.

    II Key Practice #1: Individuals ensure their own interests remain aligned with organizational interests in supporting innovative negotiation practices across the industry and with key negotiation partners.

Negotiation Capability Model at Level 4

We've seen that Level 2 creates a repeatable foundation and Level 3 allows for creativity and artistry in the negotiation process, both of them leading to far better and far more consistent outcomes. Level 4 challenges the context of each negotiation, allowing all parties to a negotiation to uncover value that cannot be created by one party alone, no matter how effective their negotiation skills.

Once again, we note that not every negotiation needs to be or should be conducted at Level 4. Some negotiations are routine, lower-value processes that are best served by simple, repeatable, and consistent procedures that deliver the needed results quickly and cost-effectively. Other negotiations are more important or even critical to the strategic success of the organization, and these negotiations demand at least a Level 3 approach, one that ensures the organization achieves its important goals at a higher level. And some of these important negotiations should also be approached from an even deeper level, where all parties to the negotiation explore outside the accepted structures and parameters to look for new ways to jointly increase the value of the deal for everyone. This is where Level 4 shines.

Key Practices Condensed—Level 4: Optimized Performance

In summary, to work at Level 4, Key Practices must include the following:

Strategy, Values, and Direction:

SVD Key Practice #1A: A partnered approach to negotiations is embedded and communicated internally as part of the organization's values and strategies.

SVD Key Practice #1B: Core organizational and negotiation values are regularly shared across the industry and with negotiation partners to advance effective negotiation approaches beyond the organization.

SVD Key Practice #2A: Negotiation strategies are expanded to include a collaborative, partnered approach with key organizations.

SVD Key Practice #2B: Specific negotiation processes and procedures have been developed to implement an interorganizational joint negotiation strategy.

SVD Key Practice #3A: Critical data and information influencing the negotiation is routinely shared with negotiation partners whenever possible.

SVD Key Practice #3B: Scorecard and KPI data is measured and tested against data from partnered organizations and industry.

Individual Fit:

IF Key Practice #1A: Individuals take a leadership role within their organization and industry to help other organizations and individuals explore the value of a partnered negotiation approach.

IF Key Practice #1B: Individuals share best practices and adaptations to the partnered approach with negotiation colleagues across their industry.

IF Key Practice #2A: Negotiators include data gathering and data sharing into negotiation planning processes wherever possible.

IF Key Practice #2B: Negotiators develop key measurements and KPIs to support industry best practices and share with key negotiation partners.

Human Capital and Organizational Investment:

HCOI Key Practice #1: Hiring criteria contains a strong component of collaborative and partnered negotiation skills, experience, and values.

HCOI Key Practice #2A: Significant organizational investment is allocated to sharing and supporting best practices in the negotiation process with key negotiation partners and across the industry.

HCOI Key Practice #2B: Opportunities for shared training focused on a partnered approach with key negotiation partners are sought and supported.

HCOI Key Practice #3: Process-oriented success measures are developed internally and shared with key negotiation partners.

Knowledge and Skills:

KS Key Practice #1: Individuals are able to demonstrate the following optimized skills at a minimum:

- Focus on pre-negotiation discussions with other parties well before any formal negotiations begin
- Able to manage and share meaningful data and information with other parties
- Understand and apply an integrative and collaborative approach that seeks mutual gains in negotiated solutions
- Actively defines and applies procedural trust[2] principles in all negotiations
- Seeks alignment of goals and common interests with negotiation partners as a primary strategy
- Analyzes negotiations to include the interests and impacts beyond the parties at the table
- Identifies all barriers and challenges as a joint set of problems to solve
- Sees conflict as a starting point, not an end point, of the negotiation
- Builds clear issue resolution processes for resolving problems in between formal negotiations

KS Key Practice #2A: Individuals share advanced tools and expert information around negotiation practices with key negotiation partners to improve negotiation capabilities.

KS Key Practice #2B: Industry peer groups meet regularly around negotiation to share knowledge and innovations key to negotiation success.

KS Key Practice #2C: Regulatory or governance barriers to part-nered negotiation processes are identified and targeted for change.

KS Key Practice #3: Post-negotiation audits are conducted that include negotiation partners, and information on improving nego-tiation practices are shared to support continuous improvement.

Organizational Incentives:

OI Key Practice #1: Incentive programs are assessed and designed in a way that motivates negotiators to explore and implement a partnered approach to negotiation with key negotiation partners.

Individual Interests:

II Key Practice #1: Individuals ensure their own interests remain aligned with organizational interests in supporting innovative negoti-ation practices across the industry and with key negotiation partners.

Notes

1 Furlong, G. T. (2020). *The conflict resolution toolbox*, John Wiley & Sons, Chapter 7 The Dynamics of Trust.
2 Ibid.

7 Implementing Alignment— Mapping the Journey

The Negotiation Assessment Tool (NAT) helps any organization identify how repeatable, flexible, and optimized their current approach to negotiation is, and as we've seen, how engineering the negotiation function with the Negotiation Capability Model (NCM) leads to better results. In addition, these results can be sustained.

As we saw in Chapter 3, there are three stepping stones in the NCM that need to be implemented, in the right order, to gain the most leverage and value from the changes and improvements the NCM brings to the negotiation process.

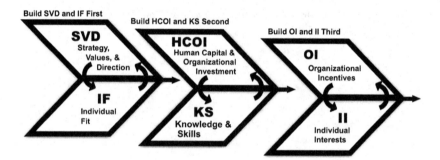

Figure 7.1 Stepping Stones of the NCM

In this chapter, we'll start by going deeper into how these three linked areas can be most effectively implemented and sequenced to achieve the best results. There are two basic processes, or journey maps, we can prescribe to accomplish this, two step-by-step road maps that will help implement Level 2 in any organization or area and beyond. What is actually being prescribed by these maps is an approach designed to meet both the organization's and the individuals' needs and interests effectively. The goal of the journey maps that follow is to give a reliable starting point and a plan, not a rigid recipe that must be followed precisely. As any cook will tell you, recipes, even though they are quite prescriptive when you read them, are simply guidelines— good cooks still vary the recipe when needed and season to taste, as you

DOI:10.4324/9781003243854-8

should when applying the NCM. These maps, therefore, give organizations latitude to choose the approach that will work best when implementing the framework, as well as the ability to choose the depth that is needed to achieve the results they are looking for. We'll look at both aspects.

First, every organization's goals are different, which means that every organization's strategy and interests may be different as well. To address these varied interests, every organization must have the flexibility to determine how broadly the NCM is applied by deciding how many capability areas need to be addressed. For example:

- Organization A may find they are deep in Ad Hockery and their negotiation results are chaotic and unpredictable across the board. This organization may well decide to tackle and implement key practices from all six areas of the NCM, resulting in a fully integrated approach. Wherever negotiations are interwoven into their business units—procurement, sales, service, project management, collective bargaining, strategic partnerships—a full court press implementing all areas of the NCM might well be needed to achieve the outcomes they are looking for.
- Organization B, however, may have a single pain point for negotiations that center around their relationship with their union and may therefore decide to focus primarily on strategy, values, and goals surrounding collective bargaining. In this context, Organization B may focus solely on strategy, values, and direction as they relate to their union negotiations.

It should be obvious that while negotiation is critically important to the success of many aspects of a given company, it is also not the only thing that's important. In many cases, the focal point or points for a given enterprise may be more limited and that means the focus for building Repeatable Competency may be broader or narrower at any given point in time. The application examples in the next chapter will illustrate this well.

Second, depth and level should be dictated by the needs of the business, whatever that business may be. Within any organization, one functional negotiation area may be quite successful and content to have repeatable and predictable negotiation processes that deliver the results needed. Nothing fancy. This same organization may find that a different area is strategically important, and having only a basic level of competence is nowhere near enough. This organization may well choose to stay at Level 2 in the first area and support the development of Level 3 or Level 4 in the second area. Following up the earlier examples:

- Organization B, by applying the key practices in a few key competence areas, finds that their collective agreement has been renegotiated effectively, and as long as management maintains this practice and can repeat it every time collective bargaining is required, it has achieved what it needs. Level 2: Repeatable Competency meets the organization's needs in this area.

- Organization A also reaches Level 2, and in their case, they reach Level 2 in all six areas of the NCM across all areas of their enterprise. But they find that this isn't enough. They realize that a core part of the business requires creative, flexible approaches with their suppliers, and in this area of the business they invest in reaching Level 3 Adaptive Flexibility in their procurement function. While other areas of the business have made good progress by reaching and practicing Level 2 activities, Level 3 is needed with suppliers for the organization to thrive.

Each organization, in addition to deciding the specific areas of the NCM that need to be raised out of Ad Hockery, must also assess the depth and level that each negotiation function in the business needs to reach to serve the organization's goals and objectives.

What is common to all approaches is first understanding and diagnosing the extent of Ad Hockery that currently exists in key negotiation activities through the NAT, then devising a planned and purposeful approach to create repeatable processes that lead to ongoing competence in those areas. In other words, reaching Level 2. That is the starting point. Once the organization and the individuals responsible can deliver on Level 2 key competencies—regularly—they must then decide if Repeatable Competency is enough, if greater adaptability and flexibility is needed, or if full optimization and creativity will deliver even greater value.

Overall, however, what is most important is that this journey to excellence in negotiation is not theoretical but practical and simple. If the path to ongoing negotiation success is seen as difficult and complex, it simply won't be attempted, let alone applied. At the end of each of the past three chapters, Levels 2, 3, and 4, we captured the primary key practices needed for that level. Later in this chapter, we'll describe a number of approaches showing applications within organizations as they apply the NCM in different functional areas. Right now, however, we want to introduce you to two journey maps, two different sequences for putting the three steppingstones in place to apply the NCM effectively.

The first journey map starts from the very top of the organization, the other at the front line or grassroots level of the organization. In a sense, all roads lead to Rome, and the first sequence sets course for Rome directly as the first step. The second sequence engages the travelers themselves first, before deciding on Rome (or some other city) as the destination. Both sequences develop alignment effectively as the NCM is implemented.

And remember, with both of these journey maps, season to taste for your organization.

The Journey Map #1—Start at the Top

Starting at the top, in this case, means starting with the very reason the organization exists—its mission, vision, and values. The organization's purpose is what brings focus, and for a comprehensive implementation of the

NCM, this is a powerful place to start. The starting point is the organization's strategy, values, and direction (SVD).

Step 1: SVD

If alignment is what brings strength, focus, and power, then alignment must be top of the list. But alignment against what? What is the focal point, the target, the goal? Every journey needs a goal of some kind, and in the NCM, that starts with the key performance area (KPA) of SVD.

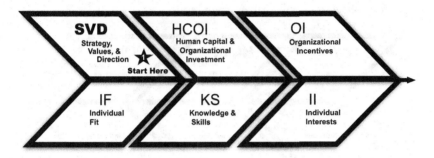

Figure 7.2 The Starting Point—SVD

SVD in an organization is both the starting point and the direction. In essence, all decisions should be grounded in and fully informed by the organization's values and by the direction it chooses to go. SVD is the North Star by which all activities are aligned. Once the decision is made to get out of Ad Hockery and start building Repeatable Competency in the negotiation function, alignment must start with clarity around the values, direction, and strategy of the organization.

Step 2: Move to Individual Fit (IF)

After establishing strategy and direction along with organizational values, the next step is to ensure the people leading and supporting the negotiation process are individually aligned with these values and support the strategy and direction.

Figure 7.3 Move to Individual Alignment—IF

Individual values need to align with organizational values, and everyone must understand and support the strategy and direction. Clarifying SVD and ensuring that all staff are a good fit with these organizational values and goals create a strong foundation for moving the negotiation function forward.

Step 3: Invest in and Strengthen the Negotiation Function

Once the SVDs of the organization are clear and communicated and the people leading the negotiation function are aligned and on board, the organization can then invest intelligently into the structures and human resource policies that will enable strong results.

Figure 7.4 Begin to Build and Invest—HCOI

These investments include a range of human resource policies such as hiring and retention strategies, as well as budgeting for and investing in the time, tools, and training required to allow the negotiation function to thrive.

Step 4: Individuals Engage and Implement the Resources

Step 4 is back to the individual level. Once the organization has allocated the resources and begun to build the negotiation infrastructure, it's up to the individuals to engage in the training offered, learn and follow the systems and processes, track the measurements, and apply their skills and knowledge to implementing Level 2 (and beyond) in the organization.

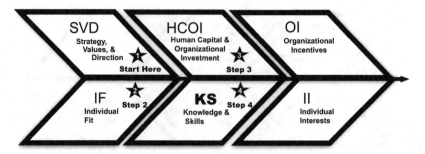

Figure 7.5 Apply the Resources—Knowledge and Skills

This can happen, of course, only if the organization has invested appropriately first.

Step 5: Align All Incentives in the Organization

The fifth step is a check-and-balance step to ensure there are no inadvertent barriers or unintended consequences from misaligned incentives.

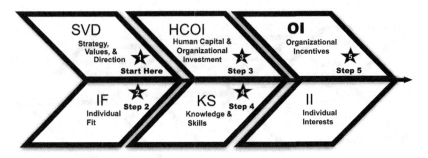

Figure 7.6 Align All Incentives—Organizational Incentives

Incentives can be monetary, such as bonuses or commissions, or they can be nonmonetary, such as career paths and succession planning. All incentives must promote the activity and behaviors of Level 2, 3, or 4, as targeted by the organization.

Step 6: Discover and Align Individual Interests

Step 6, in this journey map, is the final alignment, the final check and balance to ensure that on an individual level, the interests of negotiators and their staff are being met.

Figure 7.7 Align Individual Interests

Individual career goals and motives should be assessed and understood, and processes put in place to meet those interests on an ongoing basis.

Journey Map #1 is a simple, straightforward approach that starts at the highest level of strategy and values, and alternates, step-by-step from the organizational level to the individual level. This approach ensures that each area of alignment is built from the organizational level first, then focuses immediately down into the individual level before moving on. In essence, the implementation takes place in pairs, each pair one of the steppingstones described in Chapter 3.

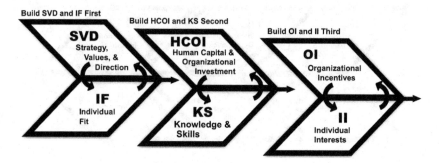

Figure 7.8 Journey Map #1

By implementing all six NCM areas, in pairs, the full range of the negotiation function can be addressed in a practical, step-by-step approach.

Journey Map #2: Start at the Front Line

We characterized Journey Map #1 as the top-down approach simply because strategy and direction typically come from the most senior leadership in an organization. Of course, many organizations engage their staff at all different levels to have input into organizational values, as well as input at times into strategy and direction. But in the end, it is senior leadership who must validate the strategy and direction, and both validate and demonstrate the core values of the company.

There is a second journey map that starts at the opposite end of the spectrum, that starts by engaging the individuals who lead and perform the negotiation function as the first step. By exploring the interests and experiences of the front line first, this information can become a key input into understanding and defining the SVD the organization wishes to go with the negotiation function in mind. In essence, we add one step to the process, a step that informs the SVD of the organization from a negotiation point of view. By adding the interests of the individuals early in the process, it will greatly increase the buy-in and effectiveness of the SVD step.

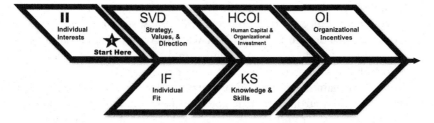

Figure 7.9 Start With Individual Interests

In this second journey map, after Individual Interests are explored and SVD is set and communicated, the implementation process proceeds along the same path as Journey Map #1: the new SVD to IF, HCOI to KS, and then OI back to revisiting II as a final confirmation on alignment.

Figure 7.10 Journey Map #2

Implementation

With either of these journey maps, the basics of implementing change apply just as much with changing your negotiation function as with any other organizational change. Attention should be paid to these basic requirements, including:

1. **Clear Sponsorship and Ownership:** This cannot be overemphasized—someone in the organization must sponsor and own the negotiation function, and someone must be fully accountable for implementing each step. In addition, the appropriate time and resources must be available to whoever is accountable for accomplishing these goals. We would offer a few important thoughts here. First, consider the idea of a C-suite position as the owner of the negotiation process in the organization. Every significant function in the organization is represented in the C-suite—chief operating officer, chief technology officer, chief financial officer, chief marketing officer, chief human resource officer,

chief strategy officer, and so on. We suggest it may be time for a chief negotiation officer as well, someone who leads, supports, and champions best practices in negotiation. It will, of course, depend on the size of the entity, but even if this title is simply part of a senior leadership portfolio, it will give it the focus and importance that is needed. Second, and again depending on organizational size, each senior manager who oversees an important negotiation function should be delegated accountability for ensuring one of these journey maps is implemented and followed by the relevant staff. Only when negotiation is seen and treated as essential to the organization's success will repeatable, adaptable, and optimized results be consistently delivered.

2. **Clear Mandate:** Clarity of mandate is always important. Here, assessing the current state of the negotiation function with the NAT helps establish the current state and the reason to embark on building Level 2: Repeatable Competency in the organization. The mandate and rationale need to be clear and communicated.

3. **Clear Plan:** Following one of the journey maps will help structure the process effectively, but nothing replaces a proper project plan with timelines, targets, and milestones. Performance metrics (also one of the ongoing competencies needed at all levels) should be set and measured throughout implementation and beyond.

4. **Needed Expertise:** Some organizations will have internal expertise in both the negotiation and the change management field to execute effectively. Organizations should be frank with themselves, however, and if the right level of negotiation expertise or organizational development skills are lacking, external help to implement the chosen performance areas and level should be strongly considered. Building an effective negotiation function should need to be done only once. Maintaining and continuously improving it should become a core competence internally.

Summary—Implementing the NCM

Organizations looking to dramatically improve their negotiation capability, to move from Ad Hockery to the repeatable or higher level of competence, should follow the pathways outlined earlier, at least initially.

In the next chapter, NCM Applied, we'll look at a range of different organizational functions and areas and how the NCM, down to specific key practices, might be implemented at different levels of the assessment tool.

8 Many Forms of Success— The Negotiation Capability Model Applied

Negotiation is an activity that takes place in almost every aspect of the organization and takes place in many different forms. Some negotiations are formal where parties jointly agree to meet, dates are set, agendas set, proposals exchanged, and the final agreement is a lengthy written contract. Other negotiations are less formal, more of a conversation or an interview, resulting in a handshake or an informal agreement. Some negotiations aren't even seen as such—just an ongoing working relationship without formal agreement on every item discussed.

To get a sense of how the Negotiation Capability Model (NCM) can be applied in a range of situations, this chapter will identify some of the many possible ways the NCM could be implemented in different negotiation situations at all levels of the Negotiation Assessment Tool (NAT). Each example will identify the negotiation process being explored, along with actions the organization or individuals might take to move from Ad Hockery to Repeatable Competency, to Adaptive Flexibility, and even in some cases to Optimized Performance.

Collective Bargaining

Collective bargaining falls into the area of formal negotiations. Parties give notice of intent to bargain near the expiration date of the current agreement, dates are set, proposals exchanged, and parties meet around a literal (or recently, a virtual) table to hammer out a deal. Here are the negotiation activities that either do, or could, take place at each level of the NCM.

Collective Bargaining: Ad Hockery

The ad hoc level of collective bargaining is likely familiar to many labor relations practitioners. It often looks like this:

- One party, typically the union, gives notice that it intends to bargain the agreement approximately three to six months before the current agreement expires.

DOI:10.4324/9781003243854-9

- A few months prior to expiration, parties agree to a set number of dates to meet and negotiate.
- Little discussion between the parties takes place about what will be on the table, who will be attending for each party, or what information or data will be used in the negotiation.
- On the first day of bargaining, parties exchange a package of demands or proposals. Parties sometimes talk briefly about each proposal, sometimes they simply retreat to a caucus room to read each other's document.
- Most parties, on the first day, set a few simple ground rules for the negotiations, typically covering a media blackout, start and stop times, and in what order they will start tackling the many issues each party has identified.
- Formal bargaining then starts, with the goal of trying to argue for their own proposals, and convincingly say no to most of the other parties' proposals. Parties stand firm on their positions. Very little discussion about reasons, rationale, goals, or objectives takes place.
- Bargaining teams are given limited mandates (if they have a clear mandate at all) and told to get "the best deal they can."

The result of this chaotic and ad hoc approach is often just a war of attrition—each party starts with as many as 30–60 proposals, stands their ground as long as possible, then eventually starts dropping their less important items until only the high priority items are left. This can be a painful process. The endgame often becomes a contest of wills, where threats of strike, lockout, or arbitration push parties to move as far as possible to get a deal. The outcome is unpredictable, with both parties often leaving the process believing the other party is behaving unreasonably.

Collective Bargaining Level 2: Repeatable Competency

Level 2 is about creating repeatable processes that incorporate the organization's strategy, values, and direction (SVD); allocate resources to support the process; and ensure the negotiators have the right incentives in place to facilitate successful bargaining. Within a unionized organization (for both parties—union and management), Level 2 negotiations may look more like this:

Level 2: SVD Aligned With Individual Fit:

- Parties do not wait for notice to be given; planning starts well before the expiry of the current contract.
- Data is collected on areas of the collective agreement that aren't working well—grievances, issues raised at the labor management committee, cost or benefits issues, health and safety concerns, employee or customer complaints, and so on.
- Outside data is collected—economic forecasts, industry projections, employment statistics.

- Organizational strategy is shared, and strategic needs for the business or membership are identified.
- Bargaining team members are chosen based on alignment with the overall strategy.
- Bargaining team members are briefed in depth on the business and operational goals of the negotiation, or goals of the local or national union, along with a clear rationale for each proposal being brought forward.
- The entire preparation process is standardized to ensure all aspects of the upcoming negotiation have received appropriate time and attention.

Level 2: Human Capital and Organizational Investment (HCOI) Aligned With Knowledge and Skills (KS)

- Bargaining team members are released from regular duties to ensure they have the time and attention to prepare for and negotiate effectively.
- Bargaining preparation includes identifying critical interests that align with the overall strategy.
- Roles on the bargaining team are assigned based on the knowledge and skill each team member brings.
- Chief negotiators ensure that all members of their team support the strategy and goals of their respective party.
- Issues from the other party are anticipated, and preparation on the likely issues from the other side is a focus.
- Lead negotiators reach out well before negotiations to discuss how information will be exchanged; to exchange proposals well before the first day of bargaining to allow both parties to prepare; to establish a rough agenda and sequencing of issues for negotiation; and to share any important data that either party will be relying on.
- Both teams commit to focusing on an integrative approach to the bargaining process.
- At the table, ground rules covering confidentiality, respect, communication, open discussion, and a commitment to explaining the rationale for all proposals are discussed and agreed before any topics are negotiated.
- Clear tracking and version control processes are in place to administer the paperwork and ensure no misunderstandings regarding what has been agreed to during negotiations.
- A post-negotiation audit on each bargaining team takes place to capture learnings for the next round.

Level 2: Organizational Incentives (OI) Aligned With Individual Interests (II)

- Bargaining team members do not have their role on the bargaining team simply added to their already heavy workload; they are given time to prepare and space to focus on the negotiations, minimizing disincentives to devote the time needed to negotiate effectively.

- Prior to choosing the bargaining team, individual interests are explored to ensure each team member sees value in participating or leading negotiations rather than simply being "volun-told."
- Time is spent ensuring alignment between the goals and interests of bargaining team members and the organization's goals with this round of bargaining. Individual interests cannot override organizational values or direction.
- The organization makes it clear that bargaining is a high-profile assignment that adds value to each member's resume.

Collective Bargaining Level 3: Adaptive Flexibility

Level 3: Adaptive Flexibility in collective bargaining will employ most or all of Level 2 activities mentioned earlier and could add the following to take negotiations to a higher level.

Level 3: SVD Aligned With Individual Fit (IF)

- Negotiation for a new collective agreement starts the day the old agreement is signed—there is no waiting for the imminent expiry of the current agreement.
- Data and key performance indicators are put in place at the start of the previous agreement, and this data is shared with the other party on an ongoing basis.
- Long-term strategy and direction are shared regularly throughout the term of the current agreement and are fully understood by both parties prior to bargaining.
- Outside data is collected—economic forecasts, industry projections, employment statistics—and shared with the other party.
- Joint sessions for exchanging economic information and other important data are scheduled well before bargaining to help each party understand the other party's perspective and frame of reference for important issues.
- Parties discuss exactly what structure the exchange of proposals will take, and what information will be included. This exchange takes place well before the first day of bargaining, so both teams come to the table well-prepared.
- The entire standardized preparation process includes anticipation and planning for unexpected issues to arise, recent changes in government policy, emerging industry problems, and so on.

Level 3: HCOI Aligned With KS

- Bargaining team members arrange mock negotiation sessions with other staff playing the role of the other party as a way to prepare for addressing the unexpected.

- Bargaining preparation includes chief negotiators having off-the-record discussions ahead of bargaining to understand where the likely barriers for each team will be.
- Bargaining team members who are assigned specific areas to prepare engage other stakeholders to ensure they have the knowledge to function as a subject matter expert when needed.
- At the table, rules of engagement that privilege an integrative or mutual gains approach to problem-solving the issues are established and understood.
- After negotiations are completed, a full debrief and audit is conducted not just by one's own bargaining team but done jointly with the other bargaining team as well.

Level 3: OI Aligned With II

- Bargaining team members are rewarded in some way for participating on the bargaining team with perks and benefits such as time off in lieu of overtime, recognition from leadership (or other forms of recognition within the organization) to emphasize the importance and value of serving on a bargaining team.
- Leadership meets with team members post-negotiation to mark individual learning and growth and ensure the bargaining experience is aligned with individual goals and objectives.

Collective Bargaining Level 4: Optimized Performance

Level 4: Optimized Performance in collective bargaining will employ most or all of Level 3 activities and could add the following to take negotiations to a deeper level.

Level 4: SVD Aligned With IF:

- Collective bargaining is seen as a critical enabler of organizational strategy. Prior to bargaining, management and the union meet to discuss, understand, and have input into long-term organizational strategy and how the workforce fits into this.
- Individuals who have demonstrated strong relationship-building skills are chosen for the bargaining team.

Level 4: HCOI Aligned With KS

- Prior to the start of negotiations, union and management bargaining teams participate in joint bargaining training that focuses on integrative and mutual gains skills at the table.
- Bargaining preparation focuses on early and in-depth discussions between teams to jointly design information gathering and proposal exchange, data sharing, and jointly retaining experts where needed.

- After negotiations are completed, parties jointly communicate the changes to the collective agreement to all staff and management, ensuring alignment in communication.
- Parties agree to some version of a "living agreement," whereby language regarding working conditions and processes in the collective agreement is renegotiated on an ongoing basis, with only wages and benefits negotiated every two or three years. Alternatively, parties sign long-term agreements (10+ years) with "living agreement" negotiations when needed, and reopeners for wages every two or three years.

Level 4: OI Aligned With II

- In collective bargaining, Level 4 practices would need to be carefully considered. Monetary incentives, for example, for either management or union leaders directly related to negotiations would likely be counterproductive, if not inappropriate. Other incentives that aligned well with individual interests may serve to reinforce a culture of collaboration, such as:

  o Bargaining leaders from union and management are funded to jointly attend and present at industry or labor relations conferences regarding the approaches and processes they used to achieve Level 4 Optimized Performance in their organization.

Summary—Collective Bargaining

In formal collective bargaining negotiations, each level above Ad Hockery adds value, starting internally with strong and clear processes that are regularly followed by the individual teams. As repeatable practices take root and build institutional memory, these can be followed by adaptive and flexible ways to build better agreements. Finally, as parties see additional value in collaborating at the table, full engagement can start to take place between the parties right from the start. Parties may begin by jointly designing the process as a way to ensure a high level of buy-in and better outcomes with virtually any issue the parties face.

Project Management

Project management is often not seen as a negotiation process, yet few roles within an organization require such a high-level set of negotiation skills in every aspect of the job. Project managers are often outside the normal chain of command and lack formal authority over the operational departments they are working with or within; yet they are expected to build support and collaboration wherever needed. Here are the negotiation activities that either do, or could, take place at each level of the NCM.

Project Management: Ad Hockery

The ad hoc level of project management is likely familiar to everyone who has worked in just about any kind of organization. It often looks like this:

- Project planning is done as a separate activity from the operational side of the business, with little input at the start.
- Project team members are assigned to the project, typically without consultation or buy-in.
- Once a project plan is finalized, operational issues are considered as an afterthought, and the project team attempts to keep it on track with little consideration given to the impact on other parts of the organization. The project, after all, is a higher priority, right?
- Given the lack of input from stakeholders, unintended consequences abound, often resulting in delays and rework that is costly and time-consuming.
- Blame abounds. The project team blames a lack of support from important operational units; operational units blame the lack of expertise, planning, knowledge, and skills on the project team.
- Projects end up in the ditch and are rebooted, sometimes more than once and with a new project leader, who often repeats some of the same mistakes.
- Projects come in late and over budget.

The result of this poorly planned approach is deep frustration on the part of all parties, a great deal of blame and finger-pointing, internal turf wars, and excessive cost and time to deliver a project. Let's take a look at how the NCM, at various levels, can change this.

Project Management Level 2: Repeatable Competency

Level 2 is about creating repeatable processes that engage all stakeholders while incorporating the organization's SVD. The right resources need to be allocated to support the process, in this case to support multidirectional negotiations with all affected divisions and departments to ensure alignment right from the start. Project leaders need to have the right incentives in place to facilitate successful delivery of the project as well.

Level 2: SVD Aligned With IF

- The organization ensures that every project is aligned with the strategy and direction of the organization, and this strategy and direction are communicated clearly to all affected areas of the organization. All parties understand the value and priority of the project.
- The core values of the organization are integrated into the project team's planning and processes from the start.

- Project leaders are chosen based on fit and alignment with core values, along with their ability to achieve the expected time and cost deliverables.
- Realistic targets and deliverables are set and agreed with project leaders and operational areas based on appropriate data and validated measurements.
- Project leaders build strong relationships and communication channels with all affected areas from the start of the project.

Level 2: HCOI Aligned With KS

- Project leaders bring project team members on board based on needed skill sets including technical skills, organizational skills, and communication and relationship skills where collaboration with functional units is required.
- Roles on the project team are assigned based on the knowledge and skill each team member brings.
- Project team leads negotiate a clear issue resolution process with all functional areas at the start of the project.
- Clear project plan processes with deliverables, dates, and milestones are established only through consultation with all affected functional units.
- Project progress and assessments are conducted on an ongoing basis with all affected stakeholders.
- A post-project audit is conducted by the project team to capture learnings.

Level 2: OI Aligned With II

- Prior to choosing the project team leads and members, individual interests are explored to ensure each team member sees value in participating or serving on the team rather than simply being "volun-told."
- Time is spent ensuring alignment between the goals and interests of project team members and the organization's goals with each project. Individual interests or individual lack of alignment cannot override organizational values or direction.
- Serving on the project team does not bring disincentives with it, such as losing promotion opportunities while seconded away from a home position.

Project Management Level 3: Adaptive Flexibility

Level 3: Adaptive Flexibility in project management will employ most or all of Level 2 activities and could add the following to take project team negotiations to a higher level:

Level 3: SVD Aligned With IF

- Except in emergency situations, projects are planned well in advance, allowing deeper engagement with functional areas and consultants as appropriate.
- Data and key performance indicators are put in place prior to the start of the project, and this data is validated with all affected areas to ensure the project starts from a realistic place.
- Agreed metrics, target dates, and activities are shared with all affected areas regularly, to ensure there are no surprises.
- Communication and contingency plans are agreed at the start of the project with all functional areas to ensure that when significant issues arise that change the project plan, all affected areas support any required changes to the timing and deliverables.
- Project leaders apply integrative and collaborative approaches when disagreements arise with functional areas or service providers to the project.

Level 3: HCOI Aligned With KS

- The organization invests in negotiation skills training focused on integrative problem-solving practices for all project leaders.
- Project leaders consistently seek to build and strengthen long-term relationships throughout the project life span.
- After projects are completed, a full debrief and audit is conducted not just on the project team but is done jointly with leaders in all affected areas of the project.

Level 3: OI Aligned With II

- Career paths for successful project managers or leads are developed to maximize retention of project staff.
- Monetary incentives, if applied, are carefully designed to avoid privileging individual interests over organizational goals.

Project Management Level 4: Optimized Performance

Level 4: Optimized Performance in project management will employ most or all of Level 3 activities and could add the following to take negotiations to a deeper level:

Level 4: SVD Aligned With IF

- Project management is seen as a critical enabler of organizational strategy. Prior to major projects, senior management, project leaders, and functional area leaders meet to ensure full support and buy-in at all levels.

- Project leaders are fully engaged in relevant industry groups to assess and bring best practices into project management in the organization.
- Project leaders share their own best practices with colleagues across their industry.

Level 4: HCOI Aligned With KS

- Project leaders are skilled at building procedural trust[1] into all project management activities.
- When working with outside resources, project leaders ensure a partnered approach is built with all vendors prior to project start.

Level 4: OI Aligned With II

- For project managers, monetary and nonmonetary incentives are designed to focus on a partnered approach to all project activities.

Summary—Project Management

In project management activities, most negotiations are internal across functional groups, and the tendency is to over-rely on the authority of the hierarchy to ensure cooperation. This approach to negotiation almost always fails, as the core tenets of a true partnered approach to the negotiation process cannot rely on authority or outside pressure. Each level of the NCM points negotiations around project management activities toward repeatable and transparent processes first, then toward a flexible and partnered approach. This same approach is even more important when external vendors are key members of the project team. Without the strategy, investment, skills, and incentives to keep all project management negotiations focused on joint success, Ad Hockery will once again take hold.

Strategic Alliances, Mergers, and Takeovers

Many organizations form strategic alliances with key partners to enhance the value each party can create and receive. In other cases, organizations merge to create efficiencies and to dovetail two organizations' strengths and weaknesses, enhancing the value of the merged organization. At other times, an organization is purchased outright and integrated into the parent company, bringing technology, skills, or personnel that the purchasing organization needs. Unfortunately, many mergers and takeovers reduce the overall value that existed when the companies were separate. Many strategic alliances fail to deliver the value the parties thought they would, and the partnership ends. Much of this has to do with a failure by the parties to negotiate strong, integrated processes or agreements that support the parties' goals. Here are the negotiation activities that either do, or could, take place at each level of the NCM. Note that these activities, for simplicity's sake, focus on strategic alliances; many can apply to mergers and takeovers as well, although there will be other activities specific to each circumstance that should be considered in addition to these.

Strategic Alliance: Ad Hockery

The ad hoc level of strategic alliances often looks like this:

- Each party tends to focus only on the value they are seeking and tend to play down or ignore the value the other party is seeking.
- Alliance agreements are often very narrow, not allowing the full value of working as partners to even reach the table.
- The alliance starts with great enthusiasm and positive sentiment, then starts to erode as friction points emerge that were not considered at the outset.
- Parties focus mostly on demonstrating a feel-good relationship rather than discussing the harder issues up front.
- Senior leadership often touts the alliance but still tasks mid-level management with protecting their organizational interest in the trenches, where friction often builds.
- Dysfunction starts to creep in, minimizing the value each party is receiving.
- At some point, the alliance dies on the vine, parties seek greener pastures with other organizations, and the alliance ends.

Without an effective negotiation process right from the start, most alliances fail to provide the value the parties were looking for, and they end despite the time, energy, and resources that were spent on trying to create them. The NCM, at various levels, can change this.

Strategic Alliance Level 2: Repeatable Competency

Level 2 is about creating structured and repeatable approaches to negotiating strategic alliances. Done correctly from the beginning, parties can create robust relationships and structures that create more value as they grow rather than less.

Level 2: SVD Aligned With IF

- The organization ensures that every partnership starts with a focus on the strategy and direction of both organizations, and this alignment is communicated clearly to all staff in both organizations.
- The core values of both organizations are integrated into the negotiation and partnership structures from the start.

- Each partner in the alliance has a senior leader tasked with ensuring both parties are creating and receiving value.
- All leaders are well versed and committed to an integrative approach to problem-solving any issues that arise.

Level 2: HCOI Aligned With KS

- Resources dedicated to running the alliance are put in place, not simply added to the tasks of overly busy managers.
- The roles and accountabilities of each partner in the alliance are defined and agreed early in the process.
- The partners negotiate a clear and strong issue resolution process that starts and stays informal for as long as possible.
- Issues are resolved quickly at the lowest levels of each organization.
- Relationship assessments between the parties are conducted on an ongoing basis.
- Basic metrics for the value of the partnership are established and shared on an ongoing basis.

Level 2: OI Aligned With II

- The strategic alliance process is focused on creating incentives for the success of the partnership, not for protecting the interests of one organization or the other.
- Individuals running the alliance are chosen based on their personal skill sets and career interests.
- Leading alliance is seen as a leadership role and enhances, rather than diverts from, career goals.

Strategic Alliance Level 3: Adaptive Flexibility

Level 3: Adaptive Flexibility in strategic alliances will employ most or all of Level 2 activities and could add the following to take negotiations with strategic partners to a higher level.

Level 3: SVD Aligned With IF

- Advanced metrics, beyond profit or revenue, are in place to help parties assess value in the alliance.
- Strategic goals and results are shared and monitored regularly between the parties.

Level 3: HCOI Aligned With KS

- The organization invests in negotiation and relationship building skills training focused on integrative problem-solving practices for all alliance leaders.
- Alliance leaders consistently seek to build and strengthen long-term relationships with their counterparts.

- Parties agree to an issue resolution process that starts informally at the appropriate levels within each organization and results in low-cost, final, and binding decisions that take the parties' interests and needs, in addition to contractual rights, into account.
- Senior leaders from both organizations regularly meet to assess the relationship as well as results.

Level 3: OI Aligned With II

- Monetary incentives for strategic alliance leaders, if applied, are carefully designed to avoid privileging individual interests or individual organizational interests over joint organizational goals.

Strategic Alliance Level 4: Optimized Performance

Level 4: Optimized Performance in strategic alliances is blended directly with Level 3. Typically, Level 4 is where the parties collaborate to create the strategy, goals, and processes they will work with. In strategic alliance situations, by Level 3 the parties are, by definition, working together to design the relationship and the processes they will use. Levels 3 and 4 are therefore, in this case, similar.

Summary—Strategic Alliance

Strategic alliances often fall prey to one or both parties reverting back to their own interests, failing to create and maintain a highly integrative approach to solving problems. Leading strategic alliances, mergers, or acquisitions from a Level 2 or Level 3/4 perspective can lay the foundation for long-term value for both parties.

Sales

Sales is one of the most traditional and accepted areas of negotiation. At the same time, it is one of the areas where the power of alignment between organization and individual goes unrealized. Far too often, sales is seen as the domain of the individual with the primary role being to persuade and convince other parties to buy goods and services or to hit sales targets at almost any cost.

Sales: Ad Hockery

The ad hoc level for sales organizations often looks like this:

- Sales goals are unrealistic and ever increasing, but often disconnected to past sales results. These are often justified as "stretch goals."
- The primary responsibility for achieving sales goals falls upon the individual.
- Most of the organizational support provided is around individual sales training and/or providing sales scripts for negotiations.

- Sales goals may have unintended consequences for the organization's broader strategic goals as the individual is primarily charged with "hitting their numbers."
- Sales are largely done within a siloed portion of the organization with minimal coordination with other departments within the organization.
- Many of the sales negotiations get centered around pricing and other more distributive negotiation elements.
- If sales numbers fail to meet or exceed goals, changes in personnel are the most common organizational response.

Sales Level 2: Repeatable Competency

Level 2 is about creating structured and repeatable approaches to sales negotiations. Done correctly from the beginning, parties can shift to a problem-solving approach to sales that supports a far wider range of outcomes: long-term client relationships, client feedback that improves product and service quality, integrated supply chains that reduce costs for both parties, word-of-mouth sales increases, industry recognition, and more.

Level 2: SVD Aligned With IF

- Sales negotiation processes are anchored to core organizational strategies and values; individuals demonstrate those values in all their sales negotiations.
- Strategic planning looks at sales in a broader context focused on strategic priorities. This is reflected in measures of success that individuals follow consistently.
- Every sales negotiation has a plan, even a simple one, that is in place and reviewed prior to a sales negotiation beginning.
- Simple, standard preparation processes are in place that require learning about prospective clients and gathering key information before any sales calls take place.
- There are clear roles and responsibilities for everyone involved in the sales negotiation process.
- Sales negotiations focus on integrative negotiation approaches and use distributive approaches only where appropriate.
- A basic scorecard and simple sales KPIs are in place that allow real-time assessment of how sales activities are achieving the overall goals and objectives of the organization.
- A peer review process is in place to promote best practices around planning, strategy, and execution for all sales activities.

Level 2: HCOI Aligned With KS

- All salespeople are hired based on experience, knowledge, and skills that align with the organization's values, goals, and strategy.

- Sales negotiators are provided regular feedback on their performance—from both an approach and outcomes perspective.
- Promotions are given to those who follow the sales processes and embody the stated organizational values.
- Sales negotiators are recognized for both their approach and the outcomes of their sales negotiations.
- Time and resources are provided to sales negotiators to ensure they are well prepared for each sales negotiation and have access to effective research and planning tools.
- Training provided to sales negotiators is customized and anchored to the overall strategy around sales.
- Sales negotiators have access to negotiation training on a regular basis and share a common language and knowledge base of key concepts.
- CRM systems are customized to support the organization's approach to sales with effective metrics, planning tools, and key data from past sales negotiations readily available.
- Post-sales negotiation audits are conducted to help identify areas of improvement both for the organization and for the individuals.
- Feedback on improving the sales negotiation process is sought regularly.

Level 2: OI Aligned With II

- Sales incentives programs are designed and tested to ensure that the right behaviors are incentivized.
- Sales metrics that support the desired preparation and sales behaviors are in place.
- Career paths are discussed and planned openly with sales negotiators to ensure retention of quality sales staff.
- Where individual incentives around sales appear incongruous to organizational goals, sales negotiators are encouraged to share these concerns so they can be addressed.

Sales Level 3: Adaptive Flexibility

Level 3 builds off the sales negotiation processes introduced and established in Level 2 by allowing additional flexibility and creativity within the organization's values and goals.

Level 3: SVD Aligned With IF

- Once Level 2 is firmly established, sales negotiators explore tailored sales approaches to meet unique needs in different areas of the organization and for different clients. Creative approaches in different sales channels or contexts are encouraged, provided they remain aligned with the organization's SVD.

- The speed of feedback and adaptation at Level 3 for sales negotiations accelerates in comparison to Level 2. Rapid improvement and adjustment should now be the norm.
- Areas for improving sales negotiations often take on an intraorganizational collaborative approach.
- The sales measurements, KPIs, and scorecards drive opportunities for further adaptation and improvement.
- Mentoring and peer reviews for sales negotiations become key drivers in learning and strategic execution.
- Individual sales negotiators are encouraged to innovate around sales negotiation processes and share these innovations for further organizational growth.
- Sales negotiators start paying more attention to the client's negotiation approaches, tailoring their negotiation strategies and processes on a situational basis.

Level 3: HCOI Aligned With KS

- Hiring criteria for sales negotiators further refine and elevate the need for selecting individuals not only aligned to the organization's sales negotiation process but, additionally, able to innovate and refine these processes.
- Sales negotiators are evaluated on all facets of their negotiation performance—preparation, process and approach, outcomes, self-reflection, and contribution to organizational innovation.
- Training resources are now well customized and refined to the organizational approach specific to sales negotiation.
- Individual sales negotiators are evaluated on their contribution to organizational improvement.
- Sales negotiators are able to negotiate with and support less experienced or weaker negotiation counterparts to allow for more creative, durable sales outcomes.

Level 3: OI Aligned With II

- Sales negotiation incentives are reviewed regularly to ensure that they support everyone following core processes, as well as demonstrating adaptive flexibility to drive further innovation.
- Cross-functional negotiation teams are established to ensure all stakeholders impacted by sales negotiations are included in the feedback processes.

Sales Level 4: Optimized Performance

At Level 4, sales negotiators become empowered to disrupt and challenge industry norms and conventions to improve strategic outcomes through the sales process. This includes an effort to impact the industry as a whole by engaging inter-organizationally in best practices and new approaches.

Level 4: SVD Aligned With IF

- Sales negotiators seek to partner with negotiation counterparts to ensure all parties are fully meeting their interests. Negotiators focus on jointly maximizing their creative problem-solving capabilities.
- Core values and a Level 4 approach to sales negotiations are regularly communicated across the industry and with negotiating partners.
- Transparency in overall objectives and the sharing of critical data become commonplace.
- Individual sales negotiators are leaders in their organization and industry in creating partnership approaches to achieving the strategic goals of both parties.

Level 4: HCOI Aligned With KS

- Hiring criteria includes identifying individuals capable of transforming their industry.
- There is significant organizational investment made in sharing sales negotiation innovations outside of the organization.
- Shared training with key sales negotiation partners is supported and implemented.
- Individual sales negotiators help to identify areas for process improvements with their negotiation counterparts.
- Sales negotiators are active in industry peer groups to help share knowledge and innovations key to success.
- Sales negotiators identify regulatory or governance barriers to partnered negotiation processes and seek to change those barriers.
- Audits and reviews of sales negotiations include key negotiation partners to better understand opportunities for shared continuous improvement.

Level 4: OI Aligned With II

- Incentive programs are assessed to ensure sales negotiators are empowered and encouraged to engage with key partners and industry groups.

Summary—Sales

In building these capabilities around sales negotiations, organizations can transform sales from a volatile and unpredictable individual activity to a repeatable level of success, from there to a source of competitive advantage and ultimately to a positive force for disruption and change.

Supply Chain Management and Procurement

Acquiring the products and services needed for an organization is a critically important function that relies heavily on negotiation. Even a seemingly stable and mature supply chain can be disrupted and can require highly skilled negotiations to navigate the challenges.

Supply Chain Management and Procurement: Ad Hockery

The ad hoc level for supply chain management and procurement functions often looks like this:

- Negotiations vary greatly depending on the individual leading any specific procurement effort.
- Deals often reflect short-term priorities and are often shaped by individual or procurement-specific goals.
- Critical supply chain negotiations regularly lead to subpar outcomes and, potentially, elevated supply chain risk.
- Negotiations focus primarily on pricing, and negotiations are primarily distributive in nature.
- Broader strategic considerations are often lost in the shuffle.
- Important data is either unavailable or unorganized.
- Critical knowledge disappears when people leave the company or role.
- Needed cost savings are found elsewhere, such as in headcount reductions, given the poor negotiation outcomes.

Supply Chain Management and Procurement Level 2: Repeatable Competency

Level 2 is about creating structured and repeatable approaches to supply chain management and procurement negotiations. Given the critical nature of an effective, repeatable negotiation process for this space, maintaining at least a Level 2: Repeatable Competency is an important target for any organization.

Level 2: SVD Aligned With IF

- Supply chain and procurement negotiation processes are aligned to an overall strategic plan that is current and well known.
- Each negotiation has a written strategy that is reviewed to ensure that there is alignment with broader organizational goals.
- Supply chain and procurement negotiations follow a specific process with clear roles and responsibilities.
- A measurement and evaluation plan is used to assess how effective the supply chain and procurement negotiation process is at achieving desired outcomes (both short term and long term).
- Individual supply chain and procurement negotiators explicitly identify how a specific negotiation ties into larger strategic goals.
- Supply chain and procurement negotiation processes support creative option generation that accounts for risk management and contingency planning.

Level 2: HCOI Aligned With KS

- Individuals hired into supply chain and procurement negotiation roles possess skills and experience aligned with organizational values and strategy.
- Supply chain and procurement tools, software, and databases are reviewed and enhanced to support negotiation processes.
- Integrative approaches to supply chain and procurement negotiations are supported and celebrated.
- Negotiation training is high quality and specifically tailored to the organization and the role of supply chain and procurement negotiators.
- Mentors and peers within the supply chain and procurement function are established and utilized.

Level 2: OI Aligned With II

- Incentive programs for supply chain and procurement negotiators are well established and tested to ensure alignment with the overall organizational values and goals.
- Supply chain and procurement negotiations leverage incentive programs based on clear metrics.
- A clear career path for supply chain negotiators is identified and in place.

Supply Chain Management and Procurement Level 3: Adaptive Flexibility

Building off the core supply chain and procurement negotiation processes established in Level 2, Level 3 is about an organizational push to further innovate and adapt these processes in ways unique to the function, organizational unit culture, and strategic needs of each specific negotiation.

Level 3: SVD Aligned With IF

- Processes are regularly improved through innovative suggestions by supply chain and procurement negotiators.
- Supply chain and procurement negotiators work closely with relevant internal stakeholders to crystallize the goals, direction, and strategy for each negotiation.
- Innovation is driven by powerful measurements and KPIs unique to the supply chain and procurement negotiation context.
- Each negotiation identifies specific metrics for success in addition to the ongoing metrics established more broadly around supply chain and procurement negotiations.
- Supply chain and procurement negotiators regularly consult with peers in the organization to share innovation and strategic adaptation ideas.
- Supply chain and procurement negotiators have access to and contribute to an easily accessible best practices library.

Level 3: HCOI Aligned With KS

- At the forefront of hiring processes are the identification of individuals capable of following established supply chain and procurement negotiation processes and contributing significantly to their continuous improvement.
- Training resources are now well customized and refined to support the organization's supply chain and procurement negotiation processes and strategy.
- Individual development plans incorporate core competencies around supply chain and procurement negotiations and leverage well-established organizational metrics.
- Peers and mentors serve as a driving force for supply chain and procurement negotiation knowledge and innovation.

Level 3: OI Aligned With II

- Incentive programs for supply chain and procurement negotiators reward both the following of core negotiation processes and the contributions to adaptation and continuous improvement.

Supply Chain Management and Procurement Level 4: Optimized Performance

Supply chain and procurement negotiations may be one of the areas most conducive to fundamentally changing the way negotiations are conducted with key suppliers as partners. Level 4 approaches can also challenge industry norms and standards that have served as barriers to more creative and effective negotiation processes and outcomes. Level 4 is about taking an interorganizational and industry-changing approach to negotiation.

Level 4: SVD Aligned With IF

- Taking a partnered approach to supply chain and procurement negotiations becomes a strategic priority and focus.
- A partnered approach is communicated to key partners and to the industry as a whole.
- All internal processes are evaluated and adapted to support a partnered approach.
- Core data is shared, to every extent possible, to further encourage and support a partnered approach with key supply chain and procurement negotiation partners.

Level 4: HCOI Aligned With KS

- A priority is placed on hiring individuals capable of taking a partnered approach and in challenging problematic industry norms and standards.

- The supply chain and procurement negotiation program is a well-resourced set of knowledge, tools, and information.
- Senior leaders are constantly driving negotiators toward a partnered approach that transforms key relationships and changes the industry itself.
- Supply chain and procurement negotiators are active in understanding and seeking to change industry barriers to a more partnered approach to supply chain management.
- Nearly every historical norm related to supply chain and procurement negotiations is questioned and challenged to ensure they remain relevant and support more innovative negotiation processes and outcomes.

Level 4: OI Aligned With II

- Incentive programs are assessed to ensure supply chain and procurement negotiators are empowered and encouraged to engage with key partners and industry groups.

Summary—Supply Chain Management and Procurement

Too often, supply chain and procurement negotiators get stuck in Ad Hockery, where they are so focused on narrow wins that broader supply chain considerations are sacrificed. At a minimum, being able to move the organizational capability to a repeatable level with more integrative capabilities is a critical first step. Still, the ability to move to Levels 3 and 4 where creative innovation and industry transformation can move it from a core competency to a major competitive advantage in the context of supply chain and procurement negotiations may be one of the areas most capable of transforming an entire organization.

Public Engagement

The public can be a forgotten party in critically important negotiations for an organization. Poor negotiation capability with regard to engaging the public can serve as a catalyst for widespread anger and damage to reputation in the marketplace. Organizations lacking negotiation capability in this space often revert to playing a public relations game instead. Yet, an organization with strong negotiation capabilities in this space can anticipate the need to negotiate with public stakeholders or impacted parties and leverage the value of their input and ideas in generating creative solutions for everyone involved.

Public Engagement: Ad Hockery

The ad hoc approach to negotiating with the public often leads to significant escalation and a heavy reliance on power-based approaches, bringing with it the costs associated with a large, public battle. It often looks like this:

- Negotiations fail to properly consider or engage the public stakeholders and impacted parties at all, causing them to seek other public forums to have their wants and needs addressed.
- Public distrust becomes the norm for the organization.
- Agreements reached often face significant backlash, barriers to implementation, or sustainability of the agreement.
- Organizations experience significant reputational harm.
- The backlash is often addressed through crisis management or public relations—trying to put a positive spin on a negative or nonexistent relationship with the public.
- Lessons from past projects or initiatives are not well understood and mistakes around public engagement are often repeated.

Public Engagement Level 2: Repeatable Competency

Level 2 is about creating structured and repeatable approaches to public engagement negotiations.

Level 2: SVD Aligned With IF

- Negotiations with public stakeholders and impacted parties are a key part of the organization's strategy and values.
- Negotiation strategy includes written plans that identify important opportunities for engaging public stakeholders and impacted parties.
- Negotiation processes have clear roles and responsibilities specifically designed around public engagement.
- A measurement and evaluation plan is in place to successfully identify public stakeholders and impacted parties and evaluate the effectiveness of the negotiation processes.
- Careful attention is paid to approach negotiations with public stakeholders and impacted parties with an integrative approach.
- Where more distributive processes are required, negotiators are transparent around overall interests and goals and in recognizing that a more integrative approach may not be possible for some specific issues.
- Particularly when negotiating with public stakeholders and impacted parties, negotiators debrief every negotiation with an eye toward continuous improvement.

Level 2: HCOI Aligned With KS

- For organizations where public stakeholders and impacted parties consistently play a role in key negotiations, hiring criteria must ensure that individual negotiators understand and appreciate the organizational value of public engagement.

- A clear career progression exists for public engagement negotiators within the organization.
- In recognition of the additional upfront resources and time necessary to effectively prepare for and engage public stakeholders and impacted parties, negotiators are supported and encouraged to thoroughly plan and prepare.
- Specialized negotiation training customized to the organization's negotiation process for public engagement negotiation is provided on an ongoing basis.
- The organizational approach to negotiating with public stakeholders and impacted parties is regularly reviewed, evaluated, and improved upon.

Level 2: OI Aligned With II

- Organizational incentive structures are well tailored to support individual negotiators consistently engaging the public in a manner consistent with organizational interests.

Public Engagement Level 3: Adaptive Flexibility

Level 2 public engagement negotiation competencies stress a consistent and repeatable approach to negotiating with public stakeholders and impacted parties. Level 3 builds off this foundation to allow for further adaptation and innovation in how this is done on each and every negotiation and to build a culture of continuous improvement.

Level 3: SVD Aligned With IF

- Processes for public engagement are regularly questioned, adapted, and improved with a focus on improving negotiations with public stakeholders and impacted parties.
- The negotiation strategies leverage intraorganizational stakeholders across an array of functions to ensure that public engagement negotiations are continuously improved.
- The measurements and KPIs for public engagement negotiations serve as core drivers for improvement and ensure overall alignment with strategic priorities.
- Individual negotiators are able to identify when existing processes are likely to lead to suboptimal outcomes and raise the need for further innovation and adaptation.
- Peers are regularly consulted and engaged to better negotiate with public stakeholders and impacted parties.
- Innovative best practices are shared in an easily accessible repository.

Level 3: HCOI Aligned With KS

- Hiring criteria recognize that the ability to negotiate effectively with public stakeholders and impacted parties is a unique skill set.
- There is clear and substantive organizational investment in technologies and tools that support public stakeholder engagement.
- Training for individuals likely to negotiate with public stakeholders and impacted parties is readily available and highly customized to the specific strategy and approach of the organization.
- Individual development plans ensure that effective public engagement is an important part of ongoing training and learning for those individuals.
- All initiatives allocate sufficient time and resources to allow for effective negotiations with public stakeholders and impacted parties.

Level 3: OI Aligned With II

- The ability to effectively negotiate with public stakeholders and impacted parties is valued across all incentive programs in the organization, with a specific focus on ensuring career paths are present to retain those that innovate and support colleagues around public engagement.
- Individuals are rewarded for proactively raising concerns around how a specific negotiation with public stakeholders and impacted parties is being planned or conducted.

Public Engagement Level 4: Optimized Performance

So often, organizations treat public stakeholders and impacted parties as a problem or an inconvenient component to their larger strategic goals. Yet there is a tremendous opportunity to engage the public in ways that promote partnership in the larger public space. Level 4 is the set of capabilities designed to drive public engagement to a partnered negotiation level and to encourage the organization to think big when it comes to public engagement.

Level 4: SVD Aligned With IF

- Taking a partnered approach to public engagement becomes a strategic priority and focus.
- A partnered approach is communicated to key groups and to the industry as a whole.
- All internal processes are evaluated and adapted to support a partnered approach.
- A priority is placed on hiring individuals capable of taking a partnered approach and in challenging problematic industry norms and standards.

Level 4: HCOI Aligned With KS

- The ability to hire individuals capable of and interested in engaging public stakeholders and impacted parties around key negotiations becomes a major point of emphasis.
- A program designed to specifically build competency around the unique negotiation considerations involved in public engagement is well resourced and treated as a key strategic initiative.
- Training is offered to public stakeholders and impacted parties to help educate them on a partnered approach to public engagement and problem-solving.
- A partnered public negotiation process is prioritized in contrast with more traditional public comment and feedback processes.
- The organization evaluates regulatory or governance barriers to engaging the public in a partnered negotiation process and seeks to change those barriers.
- Significant audits and reviews are conducted to continually improve public engagement negotiation processes, sharing these lessons with public stakeholders and impacted parties.

Level 4: OI Aligned With II

- Incentive programs are assessed to ensure those negotiating with public stakeholders and impacted parties are empowered and encouraged to engage with key partners and industry groups.

Summary—Public Engagement

Fundamentally, public engagement is one of the most ignored applications of negotiation capability. Public stakeholders and impacted parties often lack a true seat at the negotiating table and are excluded from many interest-based processes. This doesn't mean that they don't have significant impact—rather, they often resort to rights-based or power-based processes[2] in the courts, in the media, or social media to try to achieve their goals. By recognizing this pattern, an organization can incorporate the public into all levels of the NCM and transform their relationships with the public in productive ways.

Notes

1 See Furlong, G. T. (2020). *The conflict resolution toolbox*, John Wiley & Sons, Chapter 7 The Dynamics of Trust.
2 See Furlong, G. T. (2020). *The conflict resolution toolbox*, John Wiley & Sons, Chapter 4 The Stairway.

9 Tools and Guides for Assessment, Planning, and Reflection

Negotiation Assessment Tool Questionnaire

This tool is essential for the first step—determining what level your organization is operating on as a starting point.

This questionnaire is to be taken in three parts. Part One should be taken and scored first, then follow the instructions for scoring Part One.

Part One

1. The values of the organization are embedded directly in each negotiation that is conducted. (SVD)

   1—Never   2—Occasionally   3—50/50   4—Frequently   5—Always

   As evidenced by (add 1 or 2 examples): _____

2. A strategy and goals for each negotiation are crystallized and captured in writing before the negotiation starts. (SVD)

   1—Never   2—Occasionally   3—50/50   4—Frequently   5—Always

   As evidenced by (add 1 or 2 examples): _____

3. Planning and preparation are standardized processes that all negotiators and negotiations follow. (SVD)

   1—Never   2—Occasionally   3—50/50   4—Frequently   5—Always

   As evidenced by (add 1 or 2 examples): _____

4. Planning and preparation takes place well before any negotiations begin. (HCOI)

   1—Never   2—Occasionally   3—50/50   4—Frequently   5—Always

   As evidenced by (add 1 or 2 examples): _____

DOI:10.4324/9781003243854-10

5. Planning and preparation processes include data collection, researching the party on the other side of the table, and internal stakeholder consultation for each negotiation. (HCOI)

   1—Never   2—Occasionally   3—50/50   4—Frequently   5—Always

   As evidenced by (add 1 or 2 examples): _____

6. Negotiations are expected to be approached from an integrative, mutual gains approach, unless circumstances dictate otherwise. (HCOI)

   1—Never   2—Occasionally   3—50/50   4—Frequently   5—Always

   As evidenced by (add 1 or 2 examples): _____

7. The organization has basic measurements and key performance indicators in place to inform the negotiation that aligns with the strategy and values. (SVD)

   1—Never   2—Occasionally   3—50/50   4—Frequently   5—Always

   As evidenced by (add 1 or 2 examples): _____

8. Learning forums are in place where negotiators can share best practices. (HCOI)

   1—Never   2—Occasionally   3—50/50   4—Frequently   5—Always

   As evidenced by (add 1 or 2 examples): _____

9. A negotiation debrief takes place after each negotiation is concluded to identify learning opportunities and best practices. (HCOI)

   1—Never   2—Occasionally   3—50/50   4—Frequently   5—Always

   As evidenced by (add 1 or 2 examples): _____

10. Negotiators are hired based on the candidates' alignment with the organization's core values. (HCOI)

    1—Never   2—Occasionally   3—50/50   4—Frequently   5—Always

    As evidenced by (add 1 or 2 examples): _____

11. The organization has specific human resource processes designed for the negotiation function. (HCOI)

    1—Never   2—Occasionally   3—50/50   4—Frequently   5—Always

    As evidenced by (add 1 or 2 examples): _____

12. The organization budgets specifically for training and for the tools and materials needed to support an effective negotiation function. (HCOI)

    1—Never   2—Occasionally   3—50/50   4—Frequently   5—Always

    As evidenced by (add 1 or 2 examples): _____

13. Negotiation roles, responsibilities, and scope of authority are clearly defined at all levels. (SVD)

    1—Never   2—Occasionally   3—50/50   4—Frequently   5—Always

    As evidenced by (add 1 or 2 examples): _____

14. Negotiators have a clear mandate and a defined scope of authority to finalize agreements for each negotiation. (SVD)

    1—Never   2—Occasionally   3—50/50   4—Frequently   5—Always

    As evidenced by (add 1 or 2 examples): _____

15. The organization provides, or provides access to, skills training for negotiators that aligns with the organization's values on an ongoing basis. (HCOI)

    1—Never   2—Occasionally   3—50/50   4—Frequently   5—Always

    As evidenced by (add 1 or 2 examples): _____

16. Incentives for negotiators are assessed and designed to promote the organization's strategy and values. (OI)

    1—Never   2—Occasionally   3—50/50   4—Frequently   5—Always

    As evidenced by (add 1 or 2 examples): _____

17. Career progression in the negotiation function is designed and communicated to ensure retention is maximized. (OI)

    1—Never   2—Occasionally   3—50/50   4—Frequently   5—Always

    As evidenced by (add 1 or 2 examples): _____

18. The individual interests of negotiation staff are surveyed and reviewed regularly. (OI)

    1—Never   2—Occasionally   3—50/50   4—Frequently   5—Always

    As evidenced by (add 1 or 2 examples): _____

Scoring Part One

Add up the score as follows:

- First, calculate the average score for all 18 questions: _____
- Second, total the number of 1, 2, or 3 responses: _____

If your average score is 3.8 or greater for all 18 questions, AND you had four or less questions scored a 3, 2, or 1, continue to Part Two.

If you scored less than 3.8 overall, OR you had more than four questions rated a 3, 2, or 1, your negotiation function is operating in some level of Ad Hockery and a focus on bringing a number of key practice (KP) activities identified in the NCM up to Repeatable Competency is the first order of business.

Part Two

1. Organizational values are questioned, adapted, and applied in unique and flexible ways to different functions within the organization.

    1—Never   2—Occasionally   3—50/50   4—Frequently   5—Always

    As evidenced by (add 1 or 2 examples): _____

2. Negotiation procedures, including planning, strategy, and approach are proactively assessed and innovated on an ongoing basis. (SVD)

    1—Never   2—Occasionally   3—50/50   4—Frequently   5—Always

    As evidenced by (add 1 or 2 examples): _____

3. Negotiation strategies are linked across different areas of the organization to improve the quality of negotiated outcomes. (SVD)

    3—Never   2—Occasionally   3—50/50   4—Frequently   5—Always

    As evidenced by (add 1 or 2 examples): _____

4. The organization has developed measurements and key performance indicators beyond the basic level to focus on learning from each negotiation. (SVD)

    1—Never   2—Occasionally   3—50/50   4—Frequently   5—Always

    As evidenced by (add 1 or 2 examples): _____

5. The organization uses activity-based metrics that are used to help negotiators implement best practices and learnings quickly. (SVD)

    1—Never   2—Occasionally   3—50/50   4—Frequently   5—Always

    As evidenced by (add 1 or 2 examples): _____

6. The peer review process is an integral part of the negotiating process and all negotiators support and promote it. (SVD)

    1—Never   2—Occasionally   3—50/50   4—Frequently   5—Always

    As evidenced by (add 1 or 2 examples): _____

7. The organization provides high-quality training that is tailored to the organization's negotiation approach, values, and culture. (HCOI)

    1—Never   2—Occasionally   3—50/50   4—Frequently   5—Always

    As evidenced by (add 1 or 2 examples): _____

8. Negotiators are regularly evaluated on their preparation and practice activities along with their outcomes. (HCOI)

    1—Never   2—Occasionally   3—50/50   4—Frequently   5—Always

    As evidenced by (add 1 or 2 examples): _____

9. The organization invests in improving best practices, including research, technology, and administrative support for the negotiation function. (HCOI)

    1—Never   2—Occasionally   3—50/50   4—Frequently   5—Always

    As evidenced by (add 1 or 2 examples): _____

10. Career paths for negotiators are planned and reviewed regularly with negotiation staff to ensure retention and promotion of talent.

    1—Never   2—Occasionally   3—50/50   4—Frequently   5—Always

    As evidenced by (add 1 or 2 examples): _____

11. Incentive programs are designed to ensure individual negotiators support a culture of continuous improvement and adaptation in their practice. (OI)

    1—Never   2—Occasionally   3—50/50   4—Frequently   5—Always

    As evidenced by (add 1 or 2 examples): _____

12. Negotiators are hired based on their skills and commitment to integrative negotiation processes and approaches. (HCOI)

    1—Never   2—Occasionally   3—50/50   4—Frequently   5—Always

    As evidenced by (add 1 or 2 examples): _____

Scoring Part Two

Add up the score as follows:

*   First, calculate the average score for all 12 questions: _____
*   Second, total the number of 1, 2 or 3 responses: _____

If your average score is 3.8 or greater for all 12 questions, AND you had three or fewer questions with a score of 3, 2, or 1, continue to Part Three.

If your average score is less than 3.8 overall, OR you had more than three questions rated a 3, 2, or 1, your negotiation function is operating primarily in Repeatable Competency, and a focus on bringing a number of key practice activities identified in the NCM up to Adaptive Flexibility is the next order of business.

Part Three

1. A partnered approach to negotiations is embedded as part of the organization's values and strategies. (SVD)

    1—Never   2—Occasionally   3—50/50   4—Frequently   5—Always

    As evidenced by (add 1 or 2 examples): _____

2. The organization's values, strategy, and direction are shared early in the negotiation with the other party, as are the other parties' values and strategy, before terms are discussed or proposed. (SVD)

    1—Never   2—Occasionally   3—50/50   4—Frequently   5—Always

    As evidenced by (add 1 or 2 examples): _____

3. The organization invests in sharing and supporting best practices in the negotiation process across the industry. (SVD)

    1—Never   2—Occasionally   3—50/50   4—Frequently   5—Always

    As evidenced by (add 1 or 2 examples): _____

4. The organization promotes and advocates for a fully partnered approach to negotiations wherever possible. (SVD)

    1—Never   2—Occasionally   3—50/50   4—Frequently   5—Always

    As evidenced by (add 1 or 2 examples): _____

5. The organization shares all key information they have with their negotiation partners during negotiations. (SVD)

    1—Never   2—Occasionally   3—50/50   4—Frequently   5—Always

    As evidenced by (add 1 or 2 examples): _____

6. Negotiators design the goals, objectives, and negotiation process with the other party prior to engaging at the table. (SVD)

    1—Never   2—Occasionally   3—50/50   4—Frequently   5—Always

    As evidenced by (add 1 or 2 examples): _____

7. Incentives reward negotiators for taking a partnered approach at the bargaining table. (OI)

    1—Never   2—Occasionally   3—50/50   4—Frequently   5—Always

    As evidenced by (add 1 or 2 examples): _____

8. Negotiating parties jointly develop metrics for assessing the value of the negotiated outcomes. (HCOI)

    1—Never   2—Occasionally   3—50/50   4—Frequently   5—Always

    As evidenced by (add 1 or 2 examples): _____

9. Negotiating parties jointly attend shared training to bring a common approach and best practices to the negotiating table. (HCOI)

    1—Never   2—Occasionally   3—50/50   4—Frequently   5—Always

    As evidenced by (add 1 or 2 examples): _____

10. A negotiation debriefing and audit takes place after each negotiation with the other parties to the negotiation to identify improvements and learnings. (SVD)

    1—Never   2—Occasionally   3—50/50   4—Frequently   5—Always

    As evidenced by (add 1 or 2 examples): _____

Scoring Part Three

Add up the score as follows:

- First, calculate the average score for all 10 questions: _____
- Second, total the number of 1, 2, or 3 responses: _____

If your average score is 3.8 or greater for all ten questions, AND you had two or fewer questions with a score of 3, 2, or 1, you are operating at Level 4: Optimized Performance.

If your average score is less than 3.8 overall, OR you had more than two questions rated a 3, 2, or 1, your negotiation function is operating primarily in Adaptive Flexibility and a focus on bringing a number of key practice activities identified in the NCM up to Optimized Performance is the next order of business.

Negotiation Preparation and Planning Worksheet

Planning and preparation are essential steps in building toward Repeatable Competency. Preparing for every negotiation, to a level appropriate for the size and scope of that negotiation, is an essential first step. This guide will ensure that all major areas of preparation are covered.

The Problem

Problem Statement: I must negotiate with (person/party) to (solve what problem):

Timing and Preparation Plan

Activity:	Target Date:
Preparation needs to start by:	Date:
Stakeholders engaged by:	Date:
Data and research completed by:	Date
Negotiation plan, including strategy, values, goals, and scope of authority completed and approved by:	Date:
Resources and support needed:	Date:
Negotiation start date:	Date:
Other preparation steps needed:	Date:

Goals and Decision-Makers

My high, aspirational target goal:	Who is their decision-maker, or how will the decision be made?
My minimum bottom-line goal:	Influencers (Should I negotiate with these people first?):
My relationship goals:	Key party or parties for relationship building:

Underlying Needs and Interests (Common/Ancillary/Conflicting)

My interests:	Their interests (not just positions):

Common interests:

Situation and Strategy Analysis

Situation as I see it:	Situation as they see it:
____Transactional (likely short term)	____Transactional (likely short term)
____Relationship-driven (likely longer term)	____Relationship-driven (likely longer term)
My chosen negotiation style is _____ so I need to be more _____ in this situation because:	Their expected/past style and strategy:
Communication plan: In-person, virtual, phone, email, for each step in the negotiation:	

Analysis and Leverage

My BATNA[1]:	Their BATNA:
What do I lose if there is no deal?	If no deal, what will they lose?
What steps or alternatives will be better than my BATNA?	How can I engage them to look for alternatives better than their BATNA?

Leverage and/or BATNA Favors (Circle one):
Me → Other party → About even

Who has the most to lose overall from "no deal"? Why?

Possible Proposals

Options and Alternatives: Building on shared interests/bridging conflicting interests/being creative

Proposal/Alternative #1:
Proposal/Alternative #2:
Proposal/Alternative #3:
Proposal/Alternative #4:

What Norms, Standards, Policies, or Expectations Are Being Assumed or Relied on by Either Party That We Need to Address or Change?

Assumption, expectation, norm or policy, and its source (where it's coming from):	Advantages/disadvantages with this assumption or expectation:

Key Data We Need to Support Our Strategy/Proposals

Key Data:	Share? Reasons for Not Sharing:

Third-Party Moves

Can I use a third party as influence? As an audience for feedback or input?
As a partner or supporter?

Overall Positioning Theme and Summary

A short statement that sums up your underlying purpose, goal, and focus in
this negotiation:

Post Negotiation Reflection Tool

This is intended to be used regularly as an auditing guide after each negotiation as a way to support continuous improvement in each negotiation. As a guide, it should be used individually by each negotiator and should also be reviewed in a mentoring and/or peer review setting as well.

Audit and Reflection Questions: Repeatable Competency

1. How do you feel about the outcome of this negotiation? What was successful in your view, and what was not? Why?

2. How effective was your preparation? What would you do differently in preparing for this negotiation if you could do it again?

3. Overall, how would you characterize the negotiation process itself? Was it consistent with overall organizational strategy and values? Why or why not?

4. How effective were the roles and responsibilities of your participants around the negotiation? What could be improved?

5. Did the measurements and KPIs prove effective in evaluating the process and the outcome of the negotiation? What could be improved?

6. What was your aspirational goal for this negotiation?

7. What was your BATNA for this negotiation?

8. What moves did you make that you believed were cooperative or collaborative in nature?

9. What moves did you make that you believed were competitive in nature?

10. Please identify two or three key moments or turning points in the negotiation (could be positive or negative):

11. What specific skills do you want to work on based on this negotiation?

12. What changes, at an organizational level, would improve your ability to negotiate more effectively the next time?

Audit and Reflection Questions: Adaptive Flexibility

13. How effective was the peer review process in planning for this negotiation? What, specifically, proved most helpful? What would improve it?

14. What did you adapt or change for this specific negotiation? How effective were these?

15. What would you identify as a best practice from this negotiation to be shared more broadly across the organization?

16. Any missing data or information for this negotiation? Anything that could have been done differently to obtain that information?

17. How were key relationships strengthened or weakened as a result of this negotiation?

18. Did you see any misalignment between organizational and individual interests?

Audit and Reflection Questions: Optimized Performance

19. Was a partnered approach to negotiation used for this negotiation? If so, how effective was this? What might improve this approach?

20. Was data and information shared effectively with negotiation partners? How effective was this?

21. What feedback was gathered or provided from your negotiation partners on how the negotiation could be improved next time?

22. What industry norms or standards, if changed, would support an improved negotiation process or negotiated outcome in the future?

23. What other learnings came out of this negotiation?

Note

1 Best Alternative To No Agreement

Appendix
A Curated List of Resources

The Conflict Resolution Toolbox: Models and Maps for Analyzing, Diagnosing, and Resolving Conflict, Gary T. Furlong, John Wiley & Sons, 2020

The *Conflict Resolution Toolbox*, written in 2005 and issued as a second edition in 2020, is a resource for negotiators along a number of dimensions. It identifies the dynamic differences between collaborative approaches (integrative bargaining) and more adversarial approaches (distributive bargaining) in a chapter on the Stairway. It also contains other valuable models, including a deep look into different types of interests (The Triangle of Satisfaction), an understanding of how to leverage the value of relationships (The Law of Reciprocity), and guidance on why many negotiations slip into adversarial or distributive behaviors (The Loss Aversion Bias).

BrainFishing: A Practice Guide to Questioning Skills, Gary T. Furlong and Jim Harrison, FriesenPress, 2018

Focused directly on the skills and knowledge side, this book is aimed at table skills and specifically on how questioning skills are critical to all types of negotiation. In addition, it contains a primer on neurobiology and neuropsychology, and how the learnings from these fields can be applied in the negotiation process.

A Behavioral Theory of Labor Negotiations: An Analysis of a Social Interaction System, by Richard E. Walton and Robert B McKersie, 1965

This foundational book was the first and remains one of the best investigations into the entire negotiation process. It identifies cooperative, competitive, and mixed cooperative/competitive negotiations, along with strategies for each approach. While not directly addressing the organizational versus individual approach to negotiations, it speaks throughout the book to clarifying the organization's goals and strategy (either union or management, in this case) and starts building the case for ensuring alignment.

Getting to Yes: Negotiating Agreement Without Giving In, **Roger Fisher and William Ury (2011 Bruce Patton), Houghton Mifflin, 1981**

This is the modern seminal book on integrative negotiation theory and strategy. A detailed book that focuses on a wide range of ideas, principles, and approaches to engaging another party and guiding them toward a "win-win" outcome. Quite structural and detailed, it outlines a foundational approach to negotiation that broadened the more labor-focused work of Walton and McKersie.

Getting Past No: Negotiating Your Way From Confrontation to Collaboration, **by William Ury, Bantam, 1991**

This is a practical guide for negotiators that focuses on preparation and five specific tactics negotiators can employ to direct and keep negotiations on an integrative foundation. Far less theoretical than its predecessor *Getting to Yes*, it is an easy and practical book to read.

The Sports Playbook: Building Teams That Outperform, Year After Year, **by Joshua A. Gordon, Gary T. Furlong, Ken Pendleton, Routledge, 2018**

Ostensibly a book about building successful sports teams, the *Playbook* is a guide to laying the groundwork for successful and effective relationships whether on teams in sports, in business, or just about anywhere else. It looks at practical steps to create culture, alignment, and an effective issue resolution process to maintain success over time.

The Checklist Manifesto, **by Atul Gawand, Metropolitan Books, 2009**

This is an interesting book focusing on one simple strategy for implementing the alignment we are advocating in this book. Negotiation is a complex activity requiring a range of decisions followed by effective implementation of those decisions. Many times, even when people have the knowledge and skills they need, even when they have clear direction, the sheer complexity of executing what is needed is a problem. For Gawand, he proposes a simple idea—the checklist. More broadly, this book has some learnings for creating structures and frameworks that help any system or systemic approach operate effectively.

Process Consultation, **by Edgar H. Schein, Addison-Wesley Publishing Company, 1988**

This is a foundational book for designing tools to improve organizational group functioning. Given the importance of teams and team dynamics in performing organizational change, the diagnostic and prescriptive tools provided by Schein can be used, adapted, and expanded upon.

The Bully-Free Workplace: Stop Jerks, Weasels, and Snakes From Killing Your Organization, by Gary Namie and Ruth F. Namie, John Wiley and Sons, 2011

Generally speaking, problems to be negotiated are organizational by nature. Yet, there are times when you are dealing with an outlier individual who is uniquely undermining your strategic goals. This text by Drs. Namie is an outstanding resource for addressing these specialized challenges an organization can face.

Index

Printed in the United States
by Baker & Taylor Publisher Services